Never Ask For An Apology

Never Ask For An Apology

Jimmie L. Clay

iUniverse, Inc.

New York Lincoln Shanghai

Never Ask For An Apology

iUniverse books may be ordered through booksellers or by contacting:

iUniverse
2021 Pine Lake Road, Suite 100
Lincoln, NE 68512
www.iuniverse.com
1-800-Authors (1-800-288-4677)

Because of the dynamic nature of the Internet, any Web addresses or links contained in this book may have changed since publication and may no longer be valid.

The views expressed in this work are solely those of the author and do not necessarily reflect the views of the publisher, and the publisher hereby disclaims any responsibility for them.

ISBN: 978-0-595-46096-0 (pbk)
ISBN: 978-0-595-90396-2 (ebk)

Printed in the United States of America

Contents

Acknowledgments

I would like to express my sincere thanks and appreciation to the following people who were faithful and devoted to editing the manuscript for this book:

* Mr. Arthur Edwards
* Mrs. Barbara Walker
* Mr. Carsey Walker
* Mrs. Arlene Whatley
* Mr. David Whatley
* Mr. Leonard Washington, Jr.
* Ms. Alice Wood

The above individuals' immense talent and personal dedication to reading through the entire text gave me a great sense of satisfaction in the printed material prior to submission for publication. All of the editors are highly qualified with advanced degrees in various professional fields and have prior experience in editing of text and manuscripts material.

In addition to the editors, I also want to thank those who were interviewed as valuable resources for this book. Listed in the order as they appear in the book are:

* Mr. Fred D. Gray, Esquire
* Rev. Elbert Green, Ph.D.
* Mr. Larry Fullwood, MS
* Mr. Guy Crawford, Med.
* Mrs. Doretha (Dee) L. Pero
* Mr. Harry T. Statham, MS

Lastly, but not least, I want to thank the following people for their helpful suggestions in the completion of this book:

* Mr. Fred D. Gray, Esquire

* Rev. Elbert Green, Ph.D.
* Mrs. Greta Anderson
* Mr. Shawn Jenkins
* Mr. David Whatley

Introduction

According to a report published by the Associated Press, three CD players hidden under a cathedral's pews in Santa Fe, N.M., blared sexually explicit language in the middle of an Ash Wednesday Mass. Ash Wednesday is the first day of Lent, which marks a 40-day period of fasting and penitence before Easter. The irritable prank caused a bomb squad to detonate two of the devices. The third tape was kept to be used for clues in the investigation of the incident. The CD players were taped to the bottoms of the pews and were set to turn on in the middle of the noon Mass on Wednesday, February 21 at the Roman Catholic Cathedral. The recordings featured people using foul language and "pornographic messages."

Although it was determined that the CD players and tapes were not explosive devices, damage, insults, embarrassments and other harm had been done. The offending person(s) or persons knew what he/she was doing when the act was initiated. The intent was to upset a group of people who were worshiping and cause harm and embarrassment. More than likely, the person(s) who committed the offense will be apprehended as a result of the investigation that followed. Following an arrest and eventual confession, most of us can vividly predict what the offender's next action will be … apologize!

In February 2007, supermodel Naomi Campbell announced that she very much regretted losing her temper and hitting her maid with a cell phone over a pair of missing jeans in March of 2006. Ms. Campbell stated, "I felt very remorseful for having thrown the phone at someone that didn't deserve it. I have a deep sense of shame for the things I've done." She was asked, what made her do it? She responded, "Tiredness, lack of sleep and just so many things. I was being really destructive to myself … I didn't know how to reach out. It was a really scary time." Ms. Campbell has a history of angry outbursts. In the above incident, she pleaded guilty to misdemeanor assault for hitting the maid in the back of her head with the phone. Ms. Campbell is commended for making perhaps her first ever confession for hurting someone else, but the expression she gave is not considered a genuine apology.

The above scenarios typify the advent of apologies and apologizing in our society today, especially from those we call our celebrities. It has been observed that over the past few years, we have seen and heard many public acts of contrition from movie and sports stars to religious leaders, chief executive officers and politicians. Some of the expressions that are called apologies have been sincere and were presented in a genuine manner. On the other hand, some of the gestures made the situations worse and diminished the act altogether.

From the beginning to the end of this book authentic examples are shown where a person offended or harmed another and followed up the act by either making a genuine apology, made a blunder or failed to offer one at all. A genuine apology is defined as a gesture that expresses one regrets over an offense, fault, or accident caused to another. The gesture includes an admission that harm was caused to the other person or group and a sincere promise that the act will not happen again. An apology should have the following elements in order to be genuine:

 * Acknowledgement of what was done wrong.

 * Express responsibility for the actions and admit mistake or inappropriate behavior.

 * Acknowledge impact the inappropriate actions had on other people.

 * Apologize for causing pain or damage to others.

 * Amend the damage caused and state future proper intentions.

WHAT YOU WILL FIND

Forgiveness and Apology. This section shows that many people view making a genuine apology and granting forgiveness are integral parts of a real resolution to a conflict.

Reactions to Hurt Feelings. Being on the receiving end of certain actions may trigger or precipitate various types of feelings and reactions such as resentment, embarrassment, humiliation, pleasure, or revenge.

What Prompts Improper Behavior. Factors attributed to why a person may act inappropriately include: Certain people are ignorant and do not possess proper skills and knowledge to relate to others in an appropriate manner, responding to a perceived attack as self-defense, devious intentions, and the desire to attain personal attention in a public forum.

Lack of Diversity. If we were to examine all of the cases where an apology was considered appropriate, we will find that the need for such a gesture was due to a lack of appreciation for diversity. Diversity relates to any quality, state, fact, or instance of being difference as compared to our own or what is generally considered acceptable in society. Human nature is such that most of us frown on instances that do not conform with our mode of thinking or doings. Frowning is not a harm but inflicting an insult toward that person or group because they are difference from us is a harm.

Etiquette and Apology. When a person apologizes to another for causing harm it is considered proper etiquette. Proper etiquette is also about being thoughtful of others where behaving with respect and consideration of others are very important in everyday life.

Rehabilitation for Inappropriate Behavior. Experts say that structured psychological treatments for behavior problems can reap genuine results for individuals who have such problems. The therapy sessions help the individuals ascertain why he or she acts inappropriately.

Giving a Genuine Apology. Offering a genuine apology is more than saying, "I am sorry." The first step toward making a genuine apology is a self-acknowledgement that you have caused harm to another person or group. The second step entails doing something about the harm you have caused. The apology should be given as soon as the offender recognized that harm has been done. However, before the gesture is given it should be assured that the statement of apology contains the following elements: A specific statement of what was done wrong; expression of responsibility and accountability for causing harm; acknowledge that you have caused pain or embarrassment to another person or group; expression of regret for causing harm; and, indication of future intentions that the action will not happen again.

Examples of how a genuine Apology can be made. As a means to illustrate how a genuine apology can be presented to an offended person or group, six cases are revisited, and rewritten in different statements to make the gestures more authentic. The five predetermined elements for a genuine apology are used in each case in reconstructing the statements.

Interviews with Distinguished Individuals. Obviously, there are different views on apologizing for harm caused to others. There was a need to find out how certain people viewed, "asking for and demanding an apology." Several distinguished individuals were interviewed to ascertain their perceptions on apology and apologizing for harm caused to another person or group. Each person was asked, "What are your opinions on asking and/or demanding an apology after harm has been caused?"

Never ask or demand an apology. Most people will offer an apology when they have recognized that they have offended another person or group. A person offended by another person's actions should promptly inform the offender how he or she feels about the inappropriate actions. Never ask or demand an apology. An apology should be spontaneous and not coerced or requested. By not asking for an apology from someone who has hurt you does not mean that you are weak in character. It is suggested that you move on with other meaningful things in your life.

I will not ask for an Apology. During a life-time, I have experienced many instances where I was harmed (I.e., demeaned, insulted, humiliated, embarrassed, disrespected, manipulated) for what I considered occurred for no good reasons. Nonetheless, I never asked the offenders for an apology. An apology should be spontaneous. It should be as the definition says, "Acting in accordance with or resulting from a natural feeling, impulse, or tendency, without any constraint, effort or premeditation. Having no apparent external cause or influence; occurring or produced by its own energy, force, etc. or through internal causes; self-acting."

Apologies Abound

Everyday somebody is offering an apology for something he/she did or said that may have offended somebody else or a certain group. If you read newspapers, magazines and/or listen to the radio or watch television on a daily basis, you will notice people are now apologizing more and more for various reasons than ever before. AOL Entertainment News (news.aol.com/entertainment) declared that, "2006 Is the Year of Celebrity Apologies." In the article updated on December 2, 2006, 19 celebrities and politicians gave or received the following apologies:

* "For me to be at a comedy club and flip out and say this crap, I'm deeply, deeply sorry.... I'm not a racist. That's what so insane about this." Michael Richards, statements made after he repeatedly called two hecklers the "n" word.

* "Please know from my heart that I am not an anti-Semite. I am not a bigot. Hatred of any kind goes against my faith." Mel Gibson, statements made after going on an anti-Semite rant.

* I will apologize to Michael J. Fox, if I am wrong in characterizing his behavior on this commercial as an act." Rush Limbaugh, after saying Michael J. Fox faked Parkinson symptoms.

* "(Tom) came over to my house, and he gave me a heartfelt apology ... he apologized for bringing me into the whole thing and for everything that happened." Brooke Shield stated after Tom Cruise criticized her for using psycho pharmaceutics.

* "Ms. Hatcher has never engaged in sexual relations with men in a van parked on her property." National Enquirer printed untruths about Teri Hatcher.

* "I made a mistake (supporting James Frey) and I left the impression that the truth does not matter, and I am deeply sorry ... that is not what I believe." Oprah Winfrey, comments after backing James Frey.

* "I sincerely apologize (for disparaging Pittsburgh) and hope people realize that conversations can be easily manipulated in print." Sienna Miler, statement made after slaying the city of Pittsburgh.

* "But I am by no means a Farrell stalker. I had no intention of getting that close to the stage and I apologize for that." Dessarae Bradford, statements made after he was accused of accosting Colin Farrell during taping of `The Tonight Show. `

* "It's trying at best dealing with (the paparazzo's) insistent intrusions. I meant no offense to my fans, whose relationship I truly value." Avril Lavigne, after spiting at photographers.

* "I saw her and it didn't hit her. (The laptop) fell next to her and startled her. She came up and we talked to her and apologized … Thank God nobody got hurt." Denise Richards, after throwing laptop that hits an elderly woman.

* "I deeply regret the hurt (relapse into addiction) has caused Nicole and the ones that love and support me." Keith Urban, after slipping back into drug and alcohol abuse.

* "I still owe Nicole Kidman an apology (for hitting on her backstage at the Oscars). I didn't know she was engaged … or that she was standing with her fiancée." Jack Nicholson stated after making a pass at Nicole Kidman.

* "We attributed comments to Nicole Kidman in relation to Angelina Jolie. We accept that Ms. Kidman did not make those comments to us and we apologize for any upsets." Scotland's Daily Record, after fabricating Nicole Kidman's quotes.

* "I don't have anything against the group that won … I didn't mean to be offensive in any way. I love you guys. I never heard of you (but) I am your friend." Kanye West stated after jumping onstage as Justice Vs. Simian accepts an award he wanted.

* "For a lifetime, I've tried to prove how much I love her. My affair with another woman is an aberration. I am sorry. I'm contrite. I 'm stupid. Foolish.

No excuse." Peter Cook, after it was learned he cheated on his wife Christie Brinkley.

* "I am deeply sorry and I apologize for letting down my family and the people of Florida I have had the privilege to represent." Mark Foley, after it had been reported that he had inappropriate e-mails exchanges with under-age boys.

* "I have made serious mistakes and am sorry for them. I am very sorry for the pain I have caused to my family, my constituents in Ohio and my colleagues." Bob Ney, after it was learned he accepted thousands of dollars worth of gifts.

* I want to make it clear to anyone in uniform and to their love ones: My poorly stated joke at a rally was not about, and {was} never intended to refer to any troop." John Kerry, statement after making a bad joke.

* "I am sorry for the circumstances that have caused shame and embarrassment for all of you ... I am guilty of sexual immorally ... I am a deceiver and a liar." Rev. Ted Haggard, after the public learned he had a relationship with a male meth dealer.

In November 2006, ABC News published on its Website abcnews.go.com/Entertainment a list of apologies under the title of, "Public Apologies of the Rich and Famous." Two of those (Michael Richards' use of racial epithets at people who heckled him and Mel Gibson's anti-Semitic remarks) that were listed are shown above. Others included on the list were:

* In December 1998, as the House Judiciary Committee debated four articles of impeachment, then President Clinton apologized to the country for his conduct in the Monica Lewinsky affair. "I know that my public comments and my silence about this matter gave a false impression. I misled people ... including even my wife." (Rex Banner/Getty Images)

* When California Gov. Arnold Schwarzenegger was running for office, damaging allegations that he had sexually harassed women threatened his lead in the polls. "Yes, I have behaved badly sometimes. And to those people that I have offended, I want to say to them that I'm deeply sorry about that and I apologize." (Fred Greaves/Reuters/Landov)

* Hugh Grant had been dating the beautiful Elizabeth Hurley for eight years when he was arrested in a car in Los Angeles in 1995 with prostitute Divine Brown. In an interview, he was asked what was he thinking. "I think you know in life, pretty much, what the good thing to do is and what a bad thing is. And I did a bad thing. And there you have it." (Courtesy of NBC/Getty Images)

* In 1966, when John Lennon told a reporter that the Beatles are "more popular than Jesus," he meant it as wry observation about Beatlemania. At least that is what he said at a formal press conference a few weeks later, after radio stations in several states organized protests and record burnings. (Harry Benson/Express/ Getty Images)

* Perhaps the most dramatic public apology came from TV evangelist Jimmy Swaggart in 1988, after he was caught on camera with a prostitute outside a New Orleans motel. A tearful Swaggart begged for forgiveness before his massive congregation. "Please forgive me. I have sinned against you my Lord." (Rob Nelson/ Time Life Pictures/Getty Images)

* When a 19-year old Colorado hotel worker brought sexual assault charges against Kobe Bryant, the basketball star pleaded not guilty, but admitted a consensual one-night stand with the woman. Speaking to his wife, he said, "You're the beat of my heart. You're the air I breathe. I am so sorry." (J. Emillo Flores/ Getty Images)

* Former heavyweight boxing champion, Mike Tyson apologized to Evander Holyfield after biting off part of Holyfield's ear. "Evander, I am sorry. You are a champion and I respect that. I am only saddened that this fight did not go further so that the boxing fans of the world might see for themselves who would come out on top." (Lennox McLendon/AP Photo)

* Pro athletes are not supposed to knock their teammates in public. But Terrell Owens broke this sacred locker room law repeatedly in 2005, criticizing his team, the Philadelphia Eagles. After the All-Pro receiver was told not to come back to the team, he tried to explain himself. "I fight for what I think is right. In doing so, I alienated a lot of my fans and my teammates." (Tim Shaffer/Reuters/ Landov)

* Skier Bode Miller headed to the 2006 Winter Games in Italy expecting to be crowned the next Olympic superstar, and had already signed endorsement deals with Nike and other companies. He never made it to the podium in Torino, and instead had to answer for bragging about his nonstop partying. "If you ever tried to ski when you're wasted, it's not easy. Because of the way I made those comments … it caused a lot of confusion and pain … and obviously that's not something I want to do so, firstly, I'd like to apologize to them." (Alessandro Della Valle/Keystone/AP Photo)

Why are there so many apologies today? Maybe because people are now asking for more and more apologies. Hollywood celebrities and politicians are not alone in offering apologies. Apologizing occurs frequently in the sports world. In December 2006, the Nebraska University football coach apologized to the team and fans for his coaching performance in the Big 12 conference championship game. But the coach did not indicate specific areas where he may have fallen short in the 21–7 loss to Oklahoma.

St. Louis Cardinals baseball star, Albert Pujols, said he was sick to his stomach the way he was portrayed in an interview last December in the Dominican Republic and would apologize to the National League Most Valuable Player (MVP) winner, Ryan Howard who plays for the Philadelphia Phillies. Pujols stated that he felt so bad because he loves Ryan Howard. Pujols said his comments were misinterpreted when he said, "I see it this way: Someone who doesn't take his team to the playoffs doesn't deserve to win the MVP."

Sometimes when sports stars do not perform as well as expected, the fans will reciprocate by heckling them. This occurred with Michael Vick, quarterback for the Atlanta Falcons football team after a game in November 2006. Mr. Vick performed poorly during the game and as he was departing the field, several fans taunted him for not playing up to their expectations. In response to the heckling, Mr. Vick made an obscene hand gesture at the fans. It was announced the next week that the National Football League officials had leveled a $10,000 fine against Mr. Vick for the hand gesture. According to the reports, he donated another $10,000 to a designated charity organization. Mr. Vick did not offer an apology but admitted that he should not have committed the act.

What is an Apology?

The origin of apology dates back to 1533 when it was defined as, "defense, justification," taken from the Greek word *apologia* as "a speech in defense," from *apologeisthai* "to speak in one's defense," from *apologos* "an account, story." The original English sense of "self-justification" yielded a meaning "frank expression of regret for wrong done," first recorded in 1594, but it was not the main sense until the 18th century. The old form of use emerged first in Latin in 1784. The Greek equivalent of apologize (1725 in the modern sense of "acknowledge and express regret"), *apologizesthai*, meant simply "to give an account."

Webster's New World Dictionary defines apology as, to speak in defense. An apology is a formal spoken or written defense of some idea, religion, philosophy, etc. The dictionary also states that an apology is an acknowledgment of some fault, injury, insult, etc., with an expression of regret and plea for pardon.

Today, as throughout the history of mankind, apologies are offered for a number of reasons. The most common reasons why apologies are rendered can be attributed to the following causes:

    * Verbally rudeness or insensitiveness toward others.
    * Involvement in a misunderstanding with another person or group that needs to be cleared up.
    * Physical harm or damage to a person or property.
    * Children or other relatives' misbehavior toward others.
    * Late, unable to keep or missed an appointment or special event.
    * Late in expressing thanks for a gift or invitation to a special event.
    * Utterance of cultural, racial, sexual or physical insults.

Discussions in this book will be about apologies pertaining to the latter definition above ... "acknowledgment of fault, injury, or insult where an expression of regret or plea for pardon may be offered." The origin of apology is not completely clear. However, the evolution of apology as we know it today probably began in a home setting. As an example, 4-year old Bob is on the floor playing with his toys. Bob's sister, Betty, comes in the room and takes one of the toys and began playing with it. Bob responds by hitting Betty and taking the toy from her. Betty runs and tells their mother that Bob had hit her. The mother goes to the room and says, "Bob, apologize to your sister for hitting her." Bob does not know what to say. Consequently, the mother says, "Tell her you are sorry." Bob then says, "I'm sorry." The same incident can be used to illustrate the next progressions when it was determined that, "I'm sorry" was not quite good enough. The second progression probably reflected, "I'm sorry I hit you." But this statement was also found not quite good enough and the next progression probably was, "I'm sorry I hit you. I regret I hurt you." Finally, the apology gesture was expanded to include, "I'm sorry I hit you. I regret I hurt you. I should not have reacted the way I did. I will not hurt you again." According to most experts, at least five components or elements must be presented in expressing an appropriate or genuine apology: 1) acknowledgment of what was done wrong, 2) express ownership or responsibility for the harm, 3) acknowledge impact of the harm caused, 4) apologize for causing hurt, insult, or other harm, and 5) promise that you will not let it happen again.

Sometimes, an apology may have a little taste of revenge in its offering. During the late fifties, my older brother Amos had an opportunity to play on three football championship teams for our high school. One year, our team had to travel to New Orleans to play a team from that area for the championship. Our school was located in a small town as compared to the big city of New Orleans. Since our team had to arrive at the site of the game several hours prior to the kick-off, the players from both teams had an opportunity to interact before dressing up for warm-up drills. My brother related that while several players from both teams were gathered as a group, one of the star players from the opposing team shouted so everyone could hear him, "Coach awakened me from my good nap just for me to come over here to meet these guys from the country. I wish we could go out right now to play so we can beat these boys, send them back to the country and I can go back to my nap." My brother said he and his teammates pretended that the statements did not offend them. However, they were motivated more than ever to win the game and did so by a score of 56–6. During the post game ceremony, my brother stated that he and a teammate looked for the opposing team star player so they could apologize to him for disturbing his nap before the game.

For all practical purposes, an apology should be given after damage has been done. Damage in this regard is defined as insults, errors, and/or omissions we have made against another person. An apology is important for both parties of the situation because it relates directly or indirectly to the three major aspects of our lives: physical, mental and spiritual. Beverly Engel tactfully discussed the importance of apology in her book, *The Power of Apology*. She stated, "Apology has the power to heal individuals, couples, and families. Almost like magic, apology can mend our relationships, soothe our wounds and hurt pride, and heal our broken heart. When we apologize to someone we have hurt, disappointed, neglected, or betrayed, we give them a wonderful gift that is far more healing than almost anything else we can give. By apologizing we let the other person know that we regret having hurt him or her. Just as important, we let this person know we respect him and we care about his feelings. It becomes one of the most effective tools for mending a relationship. Apology is not just something we do to be polite. It is an important social ritual, a way of showing respect and empathy for the wronged person. It is also a way of acknowledging an act that can't go unnoticed without compromising the relationship. Apology has the ability to disarm the anger of others, to prevent further misunderstandings, and to bridge the distances between people. Apology is also an important factor in creating and maintaining healthy relationships. When we apologize to those we've hurt, slighted, disappointed, betrayed, or angered, the caring and respect we convey through our apology fosters love and trust. When someone does something that hurts our feelings but does not apologize for it, we become resentful of that person. This resentment can take the form of our distancing ourselves from him/her, expressing our anger in numerous direct or indirect ways, or feeling less motivated to be considerate or caring toward him/her. Apologizing to another person is one of the healthiest, most positive actions we can ever take—for ourselves, the other person, and the relationship. Apology is crucial to our mental and physical health and well-being. Research shows that receiving an apology has an obvious and positive effect on the body." An apology is not a one-way street, so to speak. All parties associated with the situation gain some benefit from the action. But bystanders and/or onlookers also gain and learn from a meaningful apology.

In December 2006, the City of Madison Wisconsin City Council apologized to a blind woman who the police did not believe was raped. According to the report, for years police and city lawyers refused to believe the woman who said an intruder raped her at knifepoint. The police even charged her with lying about the attack. However, five years after DNA connected a sex offender to the attack, the city apologized and offered the woman $35,000. The police department acknowledged its shortcoming and agreed to change its approach to investigating alleged rape cases in the future. Thank God for DNA!

The preceding case is a rarity. Our nation's police departments are not well known for offering apologies even when they should … not to mention presenting compensation for a mistake made. It took a lawsuit to force the city of Monroe, LA to recognize that the city police had made a mistake, which caused considerable distress for a former city citizen. The problem began in 2001 when the citizen spent eight hours in jail after a traffic stop in another city showed that there were outstanding warrants on his record. He thought the mistake in the record was due to a clerical error and it would be rectified soon. When he was questioned about the outstanding warrants again a few years later because of a seat belt violation, he discounted the issue. However, when he was almost arrested a third time in February 2006, the man then realized that the issue was not going away.

The unfortunate aspect of this case is that the man had the same name as another gentleman who was wanted by law enforcement authorities. Although they had identical name, the two were of different ages and different races. In the lawsuit filed in a Judicial District Court in February 2007, the victim alleged he had been wrongfully detained three times because the city had maintained a faulty record keeping system that mixed up his personal information with another citizen with the same name. In the February 2006 arrest, the man stated that he disputed the charges of outstanding warrants but was taken to a correctional center for jailing anyway. During the checking-in process at the correctional center, police realized at that time that they had arrested the wrong person.

The man stated he had gone to the police department, the clerk of court and even the city court as a means to resolve the problem but made no progress. His attorney stated that his client tried everything he could to get his record cleared up. The city's attorney said they could not comment on the issue because they had not seen the lawsuit.

An apology is a serious etiquette act and should not be undertaken in a cavalier manner. Some people who are constantly in the public spotlight drastically fail when there is a need to give an apology. Undoubtedly, some feel that the persons offended and/or the public at large should accept whatever is offered as an appropriate apology, whether it was done appropriately or not. One example can be given to illustrate this point by looking at what happened in the Michael Richards case. The actor/comedian was apparently caught off guard when two men in the audience at his appearance at the Comedy Club in Los Angeles stood up and said his jokes were not funny. It just happened to be that the two men were African Americans. Richards did not like their response to his jokes. Consequently, he resorted to the use of the "N" word in talking back to them while on stage. He used the "N" word not only once but several times before leaving the stage that night. Over the next two days there was a great public outcry for Richards to offer an apology for his inappropriate remarks. After the outcry appeared to be getting greater, Richards decided to recant his remarks made on the show. Things got worse rather than better after that. He made an appearance on the "Late Show with David Letterman," where he bungled his first attempt to apologize to African Americans for his racist remarks at the Laugh Factory. In many people's view the situation got even worse when it was said that Richards consulted Revs. Jesse Jackson and Al Sharpton so he could apologize to them for 40 million African Americans in the United States. The connotation suggested that if he offered his regrets to Revs. Jackson and Sharpton and they accepted them, and then everything would be all right thereafter. Wrong! How can two people accept an apology on the behalf of thirty-nine million, nine hundred ninety-eight thousand others?

Another example can be found in the following article published by the California Caucus of College and University Ombudsman in 1996 and updated on February 21, 1997: "People who have been hurt or humiliated often hope for an apology. They may hope that an apology from the offender will restore trust, dignity, and perhaps, a sense of justice. A thoughtful apology is a powerful means of indicating self-awareness and of showing respect for the person who was offended. But a facile and unreflective "I'm sorry" may exacerbate the situation and be perceived as rubbing salt in the wound. A successful apology achieves closure; an apology that backfires escalates a conflict.

The ombuds may help the offended party consider what it means to want an apology, e.g., as a step toward reconciliation; as a confirmation that the other party was to blame; as an assurance that repetition of the offense will be avoided; or as a humiliation to the alleged offender. A public apology may help restore the reputation of the person who was hurt; a private apology may open a path toward discussion, improved mutual understanding, and interpersonal trust. Apologies can take many different forms, and it is part of the role of the ombuds to help the parties identify their underlying interests in the process of facilitating either one-way or reciprocal apologies.

The following public snafu provides an excellent example of an apology that plunged the perceived offender deeper into the political mire:

On April 4, 1995, New York Senator Alfonse M. D'Amato, on Don Imus' radio talk show, used an exaggeratedly heavy accent associated with Japanese movie stereotypes of the 1940's to mock Japanese-American Judge Lance Ito, who was presiding at the O.J. Simpson trial. Senator D'Amato said, "Judge Ito loves the limelight. He's making a disgrace of the judicial system," and he went on to refer to him as "Little Judge Ito." The following day, after considerable criticism from colleagues, citizens, and the media, the Senator issued a brief statement that created more controversy: "If I offended anyone, I'm sorry. I was making fun of the pomposity of the judge and the manner in which he's dragging the trial out." Journalists and Asian-American groups objected even more vehemently to D'Amato's dismissive and inadequate "apology."

Finally, on April 6, in an attempt to quell the rising storm of criticism, Senator D'Amato recovered with a better prepared statement—this time presented in more formal surroundings: "I'm here on the Senate floor to give a statement as it relates to that episode. It was a sorry episode. As an Italian-American, I have a special responsibility to be sensitive to ethnic stereotypes. I fully recognize the insensitivity of my remarks about Judge Ito. My remarks were totally wrong and inappropriate. I know better. What I did was a poor attempt at humor. I am deeply sorry for the pain that I have caused Judge Ito and others. I offer my sincere apologies." (The New York Times, April 7, 1995, p. A1)

It is instructive to compare the two statements of regret. The first was a casual statement released to the press by the Senator's office, stating his regret if he offended anyone, followed by a reiteration of his criticism of the judge. The Senator personally read the second statement, in a low, nervous voice, into the public record of the U.S. Senate. The full apology 1) acknowledged what he did, 2) stated that it was wrong and that he knew better, 3) recognized his responsibility to avoid ethnic stereotypes, 4) recognized that people had been hurt, and 5) apologized for having caused pain. All six of these ingredients, except the facile words "I'm sorry," were missing from the first poor attempt at an "apology."

In order for an apology to be received as complete and sincere, it may need to include the following elements:

A specific statement of what was done. It is important to clarify the exact nature of the offense, both for the accountability of the offender and also to avoid misunderstandings. The need for an apology usually occurs when two individuals or groups do not share the same perspective—or when inadvertently or intentionally—they did not do so at the time of the hurtful event. The first step is to seek common discussion or communication, or shuttle diplomacy by a third party—such as the ombuds—can help identify and, if necessary, make adjustments to the definition of the offense.

<u>Recognition of responsibility and accountability on the part of the one who offended</u>. This admission is perhaps the most important but also the most frequently overlooked element of an apology. This is the "I-statement," the recognition by the offending party that he or she had a choice to act (or speak, or not take action) in that particular way. "I knew better," Senator D'Amato said succinctly. The offender who is a public official, a senior manager, a parent, a teacher, or another role model might also acknowledge how he or she is entrusted with this particular responsibility. Some offenses, of course, are unintentional; therefore, it may be helpful, if it is true, for the offender to explain if there was no way that he or she could have predicted the impact of his or her action (or inaction) on the recipient. But, in any case, most offended people will appreciate any efforts made by the offender to explore how he or she might have anticipated the outcome—both as an indication of the sincerity of the regret and as an implied suggestion of how a recurrence might be avoided.

<u>Acknowledgement of the pain or embarrassment that the offended party experienced</u>. A non-judgmental expression of empathy is a basic step toward restoring trust. The offender may be able to identify with the offended person, e.g., "If someone had made a joke about my religion, I wouldn't have found it funny, either." or even if the offender would have personally reacted differently, he or she might intellectually empathize: "It's understandable that hearing the bad news through the grapevine was upsetting.' The acknowledgment does not necessarily imply that the recipient's response is typical, mature, or appropriate. It may be expressed only as a fact: "I now know that receiving a prompt reply is very important to you.' But it undercuts sincerity when the offender seems to question the recipient's claims of hurt or injury ("I'm sorry if anyone was upset ..."). And it subverts the purpose of the apology to dwell on a judgmental "you-statement": "I'm sorry you're so impatient," or, "It's too bad you have no sense of humor." An apology is not a suitable occasion for self-congratulation on the part of the perceived offender with regard to his or her honesty or opinions. In Edward Albee's play, A Delicate Balance, Claire says to Agnes, "I apologize that my nature is such to bring out in you the full force of your brutality," and Agnes soon responds, "... I apologize for being articulate." (New York: Atheneum, 1966, p. 13)

<u>A judgment about the offense</u>. When the offender agrees that what he or she did was wrong, saying so is an important part of making amends. The story of George Washington chopping down the cherry tree, though perhaps lacking in historical veracity, has had enduring appeal in United States culture because of its insistence on the honor or acknowledging one's own wrongdoing. Many world religions emphasize confession. But status differences, cultural patterns, and advice of legal counsel may present obstacles to formal confirmation of having made mistakes. Nevertheless, a direct self-judgment ("I was insensitive." "What I did was wrong.") is often a way to establish common ground with the offended party.

A statement of regret. If the offender has fully taken responsibility for how he or she acted wrongly or at least for having hurt the recipient, a simple statement of "I'm sorry" sometimes may be sufficient. The impact of an apology on its audience generally depends on the context—not on the words themselves. Senator D'Amato's two statements each contained those words, but one created more anger and the other may have decreased the tension. Except in relationships with a history of shared understanding and deep trust, simply saying, "I'm sorry" is rarely sufficient. But an attitude of contrition and a statement of regret are basic elements of an apology that will build future trust.

Future intentions. These details are often an important aspect of an apology. In some situations, the apology is requested when no future interaction is expected, but even then the offended party is often relieved to hear if steps have been taken to prevent a recurrence of the offense. When the two parties are likely to interact in the future, it is helpful to discuss the offender's intended self-restraint; improved behavior in the future; how the offender would like attention brought to a possible subsequent misunderstanding; or other means of preventing recurrence. Sometimes the offender will wish to ask the recipient for forgiveness; for an acceptance of the apology; or for another chance to gain that individual's respect. An apology may offer an opportunity not only to restore trust but also to achieve a better relationship.

Finally, it is important not to overlook the means of communication of the apology. Because the recipient's response emphasizes sincerity, any form of communication that appears offhand or trivializing may be resented. In contrast, any gesture of seriousness and personal investment will reinforce the genuine conviction behind the message. The above elements may help the offended person "accept" the apology, move on, and put the offensive incident behind. An additional aspect of the communication might also help the offended party have increased understanding and respect for the offender.

An explanation of why the offender acted in this way. This component is often not the first priority of the offended party, but it may be very important both to the offender and also to the future relationship of mutual respect between the two parties. An explanation may be the most risky element to include within an apology because it can so easily appear as a flippant excuse; as a defensive justification; or as a reiteration of what was already felt as offensive. Senator D'Amato's first explanation exacerbated the controversy and the outrage: "I was making fun of the pomposity of the judge," but his second presented a point of view that everyone could share: "What I did was a poor attempt at humor." An explanation that includes recognition of the offense; the pain it caused; and/or a clear statement of wrong as perceived by the offended party, can be a means of showing more respect for the recipient by making the apology a more reciprocal process of increased understanding.

When people who have been offended say, "I demand an apology," it is helpful to probe which aspects of an apology they are seeking. Compelling an apology is usually counter-productive, and the suggestion, "just apologize and it will blow over," is generally misleading. Anyone considering offering an apology should consider the potential damaging results of an inadequate "apology." Sometimes the relationship is too adversarial; the differences are too great; and/or, the legal liability too profound for an apology to be offered or received as sincere. In many situations, a future apology would be possible, but only after a process of conflict resolution—such as mediation—that involved increased mutual understanding of parties' needs, interests, and emotions.

Cultural, gender, and age differences are often factors to consider in requesting an apology. In some contexts it is highly unlikely that a person in authority would apologize to a subordinate, that a parent would apologize to a child, or a man apologize to a woman. Deborah Tannen has cited the differences around the world in drivers' responses to minor car accidents—in Japan and England the drivers are more likely to express regret and show contrition, whereas in the U.S. each driver may be more eager to accuse the other in order to protect his or her own insurance or driving record. Similarly, women are socialized to assume an apologetic stance to the point that they often open a conversation with "I'm sorry," while men may have been taught that apologizing is a sign of weakness.

A rich opportunity for an ombuds to facilitate an elegant resolution is presented when both parties can move to the point where they are ready to exchange apologies. It is common for offenses to occur in the contexts of other offenses: whether two or more individuals or groups hurt each others' feelings by speech, actions, or omissions, or whether they mutually misunderstand each other, the offense that is first identified is frequently embedded in a history of other perceived offenses.

The elements of reciprocal apologies—perhaps accompanied by explanations and requests for reconciliation or resolution—are the same as those for isolated apologies. But the coordination of a pair or a series of apologies, between two individuals or among several groups, offers all parties a model of peacemaking and enhancing respect for each other and for resolution of differences."

Apologies sometime have rewarding effect as well as a silver lining. The case involving Senator Trent Lott of Mississippi is a good example. In December 2002, while attending the 100th birthday celebration for fellow Senator Strom Thurmond, Mr. Lott stated, "I want to say this about my state: When Strom Thurmond ran for president, we voted for him. We're proud of it. And if the rest of the country had followed our lead, we wouldn't have had all these problems over all these years, either." The statements caused a big problem for Senator Lott because in 1948 Mr. Thurmond was well known as a staunch segregationist. Mr. Thurmond ran as the presidential nominee of the breakaway Dixiecrat Party in the 1948 presidential race against Democrat Harry Truman and Republican

Thomas Dewey. Mr. Thurmond's supporters out numbered the other voters in Alabama, Louisiana, Mississippi and his home state of South Carolina, of which he was governor at the time.

During the campaign, Mr. Thurmond said, "All the laws of Washington and all the bayonets of the Army cannot force the Negro into our homes, our schools, our churches." His party ran under a platform that declared in part, "We stand for the segregation of the races and racial integrity of each race."

Mr. Thurmond eventually moved away from his segregationist position and went on to the longest career in the U.S. Senate history. Undoubtedly, he moved away from this position because he learned that there was no need to use a segregation platform to get elected to political office as such a platform became unpopular in later years.

Following the birthday celebration event, things did not go well for Mr. Lott. He had recently been re-elected to serve as Majority Leader of the U.S. Senate. His statements provoked a great amount of criticism from a number of individuals and civil rights organizations as well as denouncement from fellow congressional officials.

On the following Monday, Mr. Lott apologized for making the remarks. He said, "A poor choice of words conveyed to some the impression that I embraced the discarded policies of the past. Nothing could be further from the truth, and I apologize to anyone who was offended by my statement." A number of people accepted the Senator's apology at face value but a larger number did not. Some people viewed the remarks as divisive and racial overtones and suggested that Mr. Lott should resign from the position of Senate Majority Leader. Many individuals and group leaders, including fellow U.S. Representatives and Senators found the remarks astounding and unacceptable, especially coming from a majority leader and said so publicly. The criticisms intensified especially after it was revealed that Mr. Lott had previously made similar remarks and his records also showed that he had defended racial policies over the years. Several days following the apology, President Bush denounced Mr. Lott's remarks.

Upon realizing that he was in a very tenuous position in holding onto the Senate Majority seat, Mr. Lott offered another apology on December 13, 2002 at this hometown in Pascagoula, MS. He said, "I apologize for opening old wounds and hurting many Americans who feel so deeply in this area. Segregation is a stain on our nation's soul. There's no other way to describe it. It represents one of the lowest moments in our nation's history and we can never forget that." He also asked people to "find it in their heart" to forgive him and he vowed to work with black leaders to make amends of his mistake.

An opinion poll conducted by the Washington Post-ABC News showed that slightly more than half of all Americans felt that Senate majority leader Lott should step down from his leadership post for making racially insensitive remarks at the birthday party for Senator Strom Thurmond. According the poll, fifty-one percent of those interviewed—including two out of three minorities, said Mr. Lott should not lead Senate Republicans and forty-one percent said he should continue to lead Senate Republicans.

On December 20, 2002, Senator Treat Lott resigned from his position as Senate majority leader. He retained his elected position of Senator from Mississippi. It was said at the time that his decision to resign as Senate majority leader drew a huge sigh of relief from most Republican officials. They feared that his continued presence as a GOP leader would damage the party, especially with minority members and certain women.

As it turned out, Senator Trent Lott's apologies may have helped in the advancement of his political career … or at least the apologies did not cause long-standing harm. In January 2007, Mr. Lott was elected by his party to serve as Senate Republican Minority Leader. If Republicans regain a majority in the U.S. Senate while he is serving in the position, an opportunity is presented whereby he can serve again in his former position as Senate Majority leader.

In certain instances, it is undoubtedly clear when an apology is not offered sincerely. On February 23, 2007, the Associate Press reported that a judge in Cincinnati told a foster mother she did not seem sorry for the death of a 3-year-old boy she had left bound in a closet when she went to a family gathering. The judge sentenced the woman to life in prison.

The judge made his decision after the woman apologized for lying about how the death occurred. She had claimed after the boy's death in August 2006 that he disappeared in a park. The announcement prompted an intensive search for him in the park area. Authorities later found the boy who was developmentally disabled and had been left confined for the weekend in a blanket and packing tape.

Judge Robert Ringland stated, "There has never been a sincere concern for Marcus Fiesel. Even to this day, the only remorse is that you are being found guilty and not for death of this child." The jury decided that the woman caused the boy's death by leaving him for two days while she went to a family reunion in Kentucky. The case has prompted calls for changes in the state's foster care system. The woman, who did not testify in the case, said she never meant harm to the boy. The boy had lived with the family for only three months prior to the incident.

Sometimes it is best for our own well being to offer an apology ... even if we feel that harm was not done on our part. In February 2007, while shopping at a Target discount department store in Boston, a woman accidentally bumped into a 10-year-old girl in an aisle. The woman refused to apologize to the girl according to police who investigated the incident. The incident and refusal to apologize caused the 10-year-old girl, a group of girls with her and a young woman to attack the woman. The group hit and kicked the woman and tore off her clothes before police officers intervened. The 10-year-old girl was arrested and charged with assault and battery for kicking the 22-year-old woman in the head and stomach. The three others whose ages were 14,16 and 20 were not arrested, but police stated that they would seek criminal complaints against them. A simply apology even if one was not deserved may have prevented a severe beating.

Forgiveness and Apology

Whenever the word apology is discussed the word *forgiveness* usually becomes a part of the dialogue. When a person has been humiliated in the presence of others, in most instances he/she will become angry with the offender. The offended person is left with the feeling of resentment. What should the offended person do? Should he/she hold a grudge against the offender until he/she gets an apology? Or should he/she forgive the offender regardless of what happened? Most social science experts recommend forgiveness. Forgiveness is the sweetest revenge even if you do not get an apology after someone has hurt you. To forgive means that the offended person will give up any resentment or anger against the offender who caused the hurt feeling and move on to other meaningful things in life. Some people prescribe to the proposition of, "I will forgive and forget what happened." However, others are compelled to say, "I will forgive but I will never forget what happened." In some instances, even after an expression of a deep heartfelt apology some people find it hard to forgive. According to the Bible, when Jesus was sentenced to death and as He was being crucified while experiencing a great amount of pain and suffering, He had the conviction to say, "Forgive them, Father! They don't know what they are doing." (Holy Bible, Luke 23.34)

As I was reading the March 22–28, 2007 edition of The Monroe Dispatch newspaper, I noticed that there was an article entitled, "Forgive to be forgiven." The article was written by Joseph Capers, PhD, Director of Christian Education at Lewis Temple CME Church. Dr. Capers stated that, "Forgiving and being forgiven cannot be separated. True forgiveness is the most difficult thing in life to achieve because it is expensive. The need for forgiveness is first seen in Genesis 3 when Adam and Eve disobeyed God. Forgetting is the result of complete forgiveness. It is the final step in the process for forgiving. To forgive does not mean that we deny that someone has hurt us. It also does not mean that we have to trust those again or allow them into our heart again. We do not have to forget once we are forgiven. There are some things you cannot forget. God does not require you to forget. God does require us to get to the point where even though we remember it, it does not matter any more." Dr. Capers stated that the word "forgive" occurs in the New Testament of the Bible one hundred forth-two times.

Most people expect the offended person or group to forgive them after a genuine apology has been made. But sometimes the gesture will not precipitate forgiveness or a change in the circumstances. We cannot influence other people's lives based on our own expectations and beliefs. A young woman wrote Dear Abby for advice because her live-in boyfriend would not forgive her after she had apologized. She wrote, "Jake and I have been together for five years. He finally proposed last summer. Well, I made a mistake and complained about the ring he'd bought. He took it back, but still agreed to marry me … without the ring. I have apologized to Jake every day since for what I said, but we are now split up. (We still talk and see each other once or twice a week.) Abby, Jake refuses to forgive me and make up. I spend all my time alone while he goes hunting with his friends or out drinking with them. I'm tired of not being forgiven. I know what I did was wrong. How long can you say, "I'm sorry"? Abby responded to the young woman by saying, "If you have apologized every day since last summer and it has fallen on deaf ears, you can apologize until the cows come home and it will get you nowhere. Please step back and take another look at this situation. Most men take their fiancées with them when they purchase an engagement ring, so she can select something she likes. You were tactless to complain about the ring he bought, but it wasn't a cardinal sin. Recognize that Jake is enjoying punishing you … and the hunting and drinking with his friends would have happened after your marriage regardless. Jake has done you an enormous favor by showing you how self-centered and unforgiving he is. Please be smart, realize that you have dodged a bullet, stop apologizing and run for the hills." I am not into advice but there may be more involved in this case than what meets the eye. There is probably more that could have been added to the story than what was expressed by the young woman. Consequently, the response was limited to what was indicated by Abby. Most of the wrongdoings in the case were directed at Jake. This may be correct but there is a strong possibility that over the five-year period, the young woman may have had a history of complaining or making slight remarks toward Jake about the quality of gifts he had bought her during this time. I agree that this problem may have been averted if Jake had allowed her to select the ring she liked in the first place. However, it appears that both Jake and the young woman may gain some benefit from counseling.

According to Eileen R. Borris-Dunchunstang, Ed. D., in her book entitled, Finding Forgiveness: A 7-step program for letting go of anger and bitterness, some people feel that it is necessary to receive an apology before they can forgive the offender. She states, "Because forgiveness is about our inner healing, it is not dependent on an apology from someone else. Therefore, we do not need to have someone to apologize to us. If we were dependent on an apology from someone else, we would become trapped in a state of unforgiveness, experiencing pro-longed anger and pain (Enright; et al., 1992). Forgiveness is the gift from some-one who has been hurt to give when there is a healing. Forgiveness is not pardoning. It is an inner emotional release. Pardoning is a public behavior release. To pardon someone usually involves an authority who oversees laws by which the degree of punishment is established for each violation." Example of a pardoning is the case of a 77-year-old woman from Montgomery, Alabama who got arrested for disorderly conduct in 1951 just for walking to the front of a bus and asking for a transfer. Black passengers were not allowed up front back then. Today, long after such segregation laws have been declared unconstitutional, the charges still remain on the woman's records. An official pardon would clear her record. By law in most instances, only a judge would have the authority to par-don the woman.

When a person cannot forgive, certain factors stand in the way. Beverly Engel, author of *The Power of Apology*, listed seven major obstacles a person should over-come on the pathway toward forgiving an offender when we have been hurt: anger, fear, pride, black-and-white thinking, unreasonable expectations, judg-ment, and lack of empathy. Anger is very difficult to relinquish because many people do not want to give up the fact that they have been hurt. But once this grip of the past has been released, the forgiveness and healing process can begin. The fear factor is brought out by the offended person trying to avoid not getting hurt again. Lack of trust holds the offended party back from forgiving another. Pride or a sense of one's own dignity has been known to get in the way of some people willingness to forgive and accept an apology. Black-and-white thinking has nothing to do with color or race, but instead refers to the connotation that once a person hurt you, you should not trust that person again. The offending person should not be given a second chance. Having unreasonable expectations of others means that the offended party is too critical of others, but specifically of the offender. All of us must remember the fact that no matter who we are, we make mistakes and we do not measure up to 100 percent in everything, all the time. Once we accept this reality our expectations will move to a reasonable level.

The sitting in judgment obstacle reflects people's tendency to judge others at a level above how they actually judge themselves. Judging anything means that a person has formed an opinion about the other person or situation … in most cases beforehand. It also suggests that the person doing the judging is acting as an expert or an authority where power and enforcement come into play. A genuine practice of employing less judgment of others will alleviate most hurt feelings. While growing up, I often heard the statement, "if you judge others … keep in mind that others will judge you." The lack of empathy can be overcome by projecting our own personalities into that of the offenders. This admission shows that we are capable of doing the same or similar act. By genuinely putting ourselves in the offenders' places, we then can see how we would feel about the situation.

Reactions to Hurt Feelings

After we have been hurt, we should take the advice of Dr. Gary McKay, who once said, "You have the capacity to choose what you think about. If you choose to think about past hurts, you will continue to feel bad. While it's true you cannot change the effect past influences had on you once, you can change the effect they have on you now." Certain events and/or actions can precipitate various types of feelings and reactions. These include excitement, embarrassment, insult, pleasure, contentment, and indifference. Sometimes a person wants others to feel his/her pain. Several years ago, I read that a disabled veteran informed his wife that he was going to see their attorney for development of his "living will." As he was leaving the house his wife stated that he could get all of his possessions on a 3 by 5 index card. Her statement hurt his feeling and he told her, "That (index card) is what I 'm willing to you!" The veteran told his attorney, "I want to donate my eyes to the Eye Bank, my heart to the Heart Association and my kidney to the Kidney Foundation." The veteran's attorney pauses for a moment and then stated, "John, you are totally blind in your right eye and can hardly see in your left eye. Two years ago you had triple heart-bypass surgery. I am sure you have a bad kidney because you are currently getting dialysis treatment three days a week." He then asked the veteran, "Why in the world would you want to donate your impaired organs to someone else?" The veteran responded by saying, "I just wanted someone else to see how I feel with all of these health problems."

I have formed an opinion through experience that most people with sound minds do not want to insult, humiliate, or embarrass another person, in order to cause hurt feelings. Mary was upset with her husband Paul because he always embarrassed her in front of other members of the community social club. At the monthly meetings, Paul would talk loudly to other members at their table while the chairman or other speaker had the floor. He would speak so loud that everybody's attention would be directed toward Paul instead of the speaker up front. Finally, Mary advised Paul that she would not be going to any future meetings with him if he continued his disrespect toward her and others. Paul agreed he would be respectful of her and others and would limit his talking to appropriate times. At the next meeting, when the floor was opened for other discussions, Paul was given permission to make comments. He said, "I offer my apology to our chairman, all of our previous guest speakers for disturbing them while they had the floor. I also want to apologize to my wife Mary, publicly for embarrassing her in front of her friends and others."

People react differently to their feelings as a result of certain events. As example, I read in another case where a woman isolated herself from her husband for five days because she was feeling unhappy about how things were going at the house. On the sixth day the husband confronted her and asked what was the problem. Her response was that she was just unhappy with the way things were going. The husband responded by saying, "you have a roof over your head and food on the table. Two out of three things in life are not bad." The wife's feelings were very much hurt even more so by the husband's statement and she subsequently left home altogether.

Some people have the urge to get even with the person who insulted or hurt them. But, as John Honeyfeld said, "The only people you should ever want to get 'even' with are those who have helped you." In some cases, the feeling in reaction to an event or imaginary event may precipitate violence. A man in the local community was indicted in November 2006 for setting his girl friend on fire because he felt she was unfaithful to him. He was charged with one count of attempted second-degree murder and one count of false imprisonment. Monroe city police said that the couple had an argument after returning home from a party and the man accused the 23-year-old woman of cheating and threatened to kill her. The man's feelings were hurt when he thought he saw the woman making "eyes" with another man at the party.

An apology offered to a race of people, a religious faith, a specific age or any other special group due to a presumed or actual insult, resentment, or indifference, will never be fully acceptable to all affected by the gesture. There are several examples. In March 2000, Pope John Paul II publicly asked God's forgiveness for sins of Roman Catholics through the ages, including wrongs inflicted on Jews, women and minorities. Immediately following the gesture, Jewish leaders indicated that they welcomed the Pope's apologies for past misdeeds of the Catholic Church but were disappointed that the Pope did not specifically mention the church's role in the Holocaust. Israel's Chief Rabbi, Israel Meir Lau, said he hoped the Pope would make a more specific apology during his pilgrimage to the

Israel later that month when he visits the country. The Rabbi was disappointed that the Pope had made no mention of the Holocaust or the controversial role of Pope Pius XII, who many Jews believed turned a blind eye to the Nazi death camps. Rabbi David Rosen, head of the Jerusalem office of the Anti-Defamation League of B'nai B'rith, said that it was "a little unrealistic" to expect the Pope to say more. Rabbi Marvin Hier, dean and founder of the Simon Wiesenthal Center in Los Angeles also welcomed the Pope's apology but felt that it would have been more significant if he had made mention of the Holocaust.

In September 2006, Pope Benedict XVI, in a speech to professors in Germany as he quoted 14th-century Byzantine emperor Manuel II Paleologus, stated in part, "Show me just what Mohammed brought that was new, and there you will find things only evil and inhuman, such as his command to spread by the sword the faith he preached." The remarks immediately caused an offence to Muslims around the world. The Pope apologized by saying he was deeply sorry for the reactions in some countries to passages of his address, which were considered offensive to the sensibility of Muslims. He reiterated that his quotation was from a medieval text and did not in any way express his personal thought. He also stated in his apology that the Cardinal Secretary of State had published a statement in that regard as a means to explain the true meaning of his words. The Pope thought his apology and publication of a statement by the Cardinal Secretary of State explaining the meaning of the words he used would appease those who were hurt and offended by them. The apology and clarification of the remarks did not ameliorate the situation. The personal apology by Pope Benedict XVI failed to quell Muslim fury as protests continued by a great degree two days after his gesture. News reports indicated that more than 1,000 protesters were in the streets of Basra in southern Iraq to condemn the Pope for his comments relating to Mohammed. Other reactions to the remarks included threats against the Pope and what some called, "worshipers of the cross" by an al-Qaeda linked militant group and the killings in Somalia.

In the spring of 1932, the U.S. Public Health Service began recruiting black men in rural Alabama for a study to see how syphilis would progress in black men. The study, which has since been known as the Tuskegee Study of Untreated Syphilis in the Negro Male, lasted from 1932 to 1972. The study involved 600 black men, 399 of who had syphilis and 201 of who did not. The men participating in the experiment received free meals, medical care and burial expenses. The men who had syphilis were told by Public Health Service (now known as the Centers for Disease Control and Prevention) officials only that they had "bad blood" and would receive treatment, but they were given only placebos. The men were denied access to treatment even for years after penicillin had come into use in 1947. By the time the study was exposed in 1972, 28 men had died from the syphilis complications, 100 others were dead of related complications, at least 40 wives had been infected and 19 children had contracted the disease at birth. Attorney Fred D. Gray, who represented the group in a class-action lawsuit, won an out-of-court settlement in the mid-1970s, with the federal government agreeing to pay $10 million in compensation. The agreement also included lifetime health care for the participants and for certain family members.

On May 16, 1997, President Bill Clinton apologized to the eight Tuskegee survivors, their families, and the families of those who had died as a result of participating in the syphilis study. President Clinton stated, "What was done cannot be undone, but we can end the silence. We can stop turning our heads away, we can look at you, in the eye, and finally say, on behalf of the American people, what the United States government did was shameful, and I am sorry." Although reasonable compensation was given and a meaningful apology was made, many of the family members of the study group and others feel that nothing would heal the wounds caused by the misleading information and the study itself.

During an on-set quarrel with co-star Patrick Dempsey, of ABC's television program, "Grey's Anatomy," actor Isaiah Washington used the slur word "faggot" in reference to co-star T.R. Knight. According to news reports the incident occurred in October 2006. After being criticized by the Gay & Lesbian Against Defamation and ABC television, Mr. Washington issued an apology. He also met with the heads of GLAAD and Gay, Lesbian and Straight Education Network. Appearing at the Golden Globes, Mr. Washington denied using the word. He said, "No, I did not call T.R. Knight a faggot. Never happened, never happened." ABC officials thought they had effectively resolved the issue in October but found themselves in a tenuous situation again following the program on January 18, 2007. However, after a great outcry from gay and lesbian groups, ABC television was forced to issue a statement. The network's statement stated, "We are greatly dismayed that Mr. Washington chose to use inappropriate language at the Golden Globes, language that he himself deemed 'unfortunate' in his previous public apology. His actions are unacceptable and are being addressed." It was reported that the network had strongly encouraged Mr. Washington to make a more specific apology. Consequently, he stated, "I apologize to T.R., my colleagues, the fans of the show and especially the lesbian and gay community for using a word that is unacceptable in any context or circumstance. I marred what should have been a perfect night for everyone who works on 'Grey Anatomy.' I can neither defend nor explain my behavior. I can also no longer deny to myself that there are issues I obviously need to examine within my own soul, and I've asked for help." On January 24, 2007, Mr. Washington announced that he was undergoing treatment to transform his "negative actions into positive results." His statement to the public was, "With the support of my family and friends, I have begun counseling. I regard this as a necessary step toward understanding why I did what I did and making sure it never happens again. I appreciate the fact that I have been given this opportunity and I remain committed to transforming my negative action into positive results, personally and professionally." The apologies, re-apologies, meetings with offended gay-rights groups, re-apologies again, and finally, even rehabilitation, were not sufficient to quell public dissatisfaction over the demeaning statement made by Mr. Washington.

What Prompts Improper Behavior?

Upon attending college we recognized that students who are pursuing a major in a field that deals with people will be required to take at least one course in psychology. In the psychology class we recognized that a great amount of emphasis was placed on human behavior. Of course, this phenomenon was designed this way in order for us to attain a better understanding of the way we act and/or react in dealing with others and our environment. Human behavior relates to the way we act, our conduct and manners as we interact with others. Behavioral Scientists such as sociologists, psychologists, anthropologists and social Workers, spend a considerable amount of their time examining human activities in an attempt to discover whether there are patterns in our interactions and formulate rules about our social behavior.

When a person does or says something that is unexpected, irregular, or different from what is considered normal or predictable state of affairs, we generally label the act abnormal. In social life all of our everyday activities in interacting with others are determined or judged by what is considered normal or predictable. When we fail to act according to these social expectations, we call it deviance. Consequently, labeling a person as abnormal is a social act within a definite context of time, place, and person. In the U.S., it is considered normal for a person to drive his car on the right side of the highway where the roadway has been designated as two-way traffic. Over the years certain actions at one time were considered abnormal but now are considered normal because the predictability of the state of affairs or expectations have changed. As example, forty years ago it was considered abnormal for a high school male student to sit in class wearing a cap on during the class period. Presently, it is acceptable and most teachers acquiesce to the practice. Some of the teachers are from the "old school" and will not accept it. Consequently, it is safe to say that abnormality can vary from place to place, time to time, and person to person.

An attempt to differentiate between normal people and those that may be labeled abnormal from a practical or research perspective will not be made in this book. Further, there will not be an attempt to provide an in-depth discussion of terms such as mental illness, maladjustment, and psychiatric diagnosis. Supplemental study beyond the information in this book is recommended for those who have an interest in learning more about abnormal behavior. The primary focus of the apology cases presented in this book will be that the actions surrounding the gestures were or were not considered normal based on society's predetermined appropriateness or predictability.

The primary root, which necessitates an apology, almost always emerge from a harm or insult to someone's or group feelings. There are certain forces in life. A person's feelings are one of them. Feelings are personal emotions or sensitivities where everyone has ownership. It's unalterable tide sweeps all people along its unrelenting path. In observing human nature in today's world, it is easier to criticize or insult another person or group than it is to apologize. Literally, this is true. It takes no research, study, background checks or anything else to criticize or insult another person. All the offending person has to do is articulate a few ill thought-out words or behave in a disrespectful or arrogant way toward another person or group. On the other hand, apologizing to someone or a group requires some careful thoughts and serious preparations if it is going to be done correctly. I was told that even animals have feelings! However, this book is about people's feelings and their reactions wherefrom.

A considerable number of articles and books have been written on the subjects of apologies and apologizing. This phenomenon is primarily due to the fact that we are now witnessing more and more instances where people are making apologies and/or feel that an apology should be offered. A majority of the articles and books on apology and apologizing describe the importance of giving and accepting the gesture. The articles contain information regarding what constitute a genuine apology, how one should be given, forgiveness, accepting and asking for an apology. There are several publications in circulation that list what are considered the most famous apologies that have been made over time. Of all the information that has been published about apologies and apologizing, very little has been written about what prompts an offender to insult and/or cause harm to another person or group, which precipitates a need to apologize. When a person hurts a person's or group's feelings because of what he or she said or did, generally the action had an overt or underlining cause.

In considering all of the possible factors that may attributed to why a person would act inappropriately, we must first recognize that some people are ignorant and do not possess proper skills and knowledge to relate to people in an acceptable manner. If you asked a person in this category the question, "What do you think is worst, ignorance or apathy?" You probably will receive the answer, "I don't know and I don't care!" The second factor relates to ill preparations and off-handed articulated expressions and/or actions pertaining to others, which have insulted a great number of people. This factor is not limited to professional entertainers and politicians. Responding to a perceived attack by the other person is a third factor that gives rise to improper actions. In this case, the offender feels that his or her humiliating response was in self-defense. Fourthly, devious intentions have caused numerous injustices throughout our country's history and the entire world.

The first two factors, which may prompt improper behavior, are considered unintentional whereas the last two are undoubtedly seen as purposeful. By analyzing some of the issues discussed above, we can place each of them in one of the categories. The case involving boxer Mike Tyson in June 1997 in which he bits off a part of Evander Holyfield's ear can safely be placed in the first category. In this case it is unquestionable clear that Mr. Tyson does not posses proper skills to relate to others by his improper actions in the boxing ring. Another incident to support this assessment of Mr. Tyson is the fact that he attacked the drivers in an accident on the Maryland freeway because of an unintentional accident. If he had possessed the required skills and knowledge to relate to others, such vicious actions would not have occurred.

Remarks made by Pope Benedict XVI relating to Mohammed can be assigned to the second category. Although the Pope's statements were quotations from a medieval text, which were not personal thoughts of the Pope, the remarks were made in such a way that they were considered offensive to the sensibility of Muslims around the world. All of us have to remember that people of certain religious faiths are more sensitive than others. The Muslims faith is one of them. I am neither Catholics nor Muslims, but consider myself a Christian and I strongly believe that Pope Benedict XVI did not want to insult or hurt any people of the Muslims faith when he made his speech on that day in Germany. I am sure if he had an opportunity to make this speech again he would use another quote or none at all, especially one that may relate to Mohammed in some way. The Pope and the Vatican tried very hard to put the issue behind them. A week after the statements were made, the Vatican issued a statement that said the comment about holy war made during the pontiff's visit to Germany was meant to prompt a "genuine dialogue of cultures and religions so urgently needed today." The Rev. Alistair Sear, a church historian, says the remarks were taken out of context. He said, "These statements were made in an academic environment at Regensburg University as a part of a nuanced debate. Of course it will be misinterpreted if part of it is isolated or if the comments are looked at in different context."

The reactions demonstrated by Michael Richards can be placed in the third category. According to news reports, Mr. Richards had been heckled after telling a few jokes at the comedy club in Los Angeles. Mr. Richards responded to the heckling by shouting racial epithets at the people (two black men) whom he thought were attacking him. As a long-time actor and stand-up comedian, Richards should have had the skills and knowledge to deal with this type of situation in a better way. Entertainers such as comedians and comediennes have always been subjected to harsh responses by people in their audiences. As mentioned above, Mr. Richards made several apologies ... maybe too many for the remarks he made in response to the heckling he received that night.

The Syphilis study conducted by the Centers for Disease Control and Prevention of more than 400 poor African American men in Tuskegee, Alabama with syphilis between 1932 and 1972 can easily be placed in the last category. Government researchers purposefully did not treat 399 black men with syphilis in order to study how the disease is spread and how it may kill. A lawsuit associated with the study resulted in changes made to the protocol on how research can be performed involving human subjects. Despite a genuine apology expressed by the President of the United States in 1997, the trauma of the experience by the victims and their families and the manner in which the study was conducted continue to presents deep suspicion of official medical studies among minorities. According to public health experts, blacks are the least to volunteer to participate in any type of medical studies ... primarily because of the syphilis study.

There may be a fifth category, which would include people who are seeking personal attention in a public forum. We experienced a case of this type in the Department of Veterans Affairs Medical Centers in Tuskegee and Montgomery, Alabama when we were in the process of merging the two medical centers into one organization during the late 1990s. Congressman Bob Riley held a town-hall meeting in Tuskegee, AL because he had received a number of complaint letters from people in his congressional district regarding unfairness of the merger process. It had been said that Congressman Terry Everett had taken matters into his own hands, was micromanaging the merger, and was in the process of shifting most of the resources to the Montgomery Campus which was located within Congressman Terry Everett's congressional district. People in attendance at the meeting were allowed to ask questions after all of the presentations had been made. An elderly gentleman from the community was allowed to pose his questions regarding issues discussed. He did not have a question but stated, "I have received information that Mr. Clay was sent to Tuskegee to close down the Tuskegee VA Medical Center. I also heard that he returned several hundred-thousand dollars to the VA office in Washington that was badly needed at the facility but instead were returned so he would receive special recognition for saving government funds." Of course, those statements were not even close to being true. The gentleman, whom I had met at several other community events wanted to attract the audience's attention toward himself and had no thought or consideration for the event of the merger. The next day, I sent a letter to inform him that his comments were baseless and I did not sincerely understand why the statements were made in that particular forum. The very next time I saw him in public, he apologized for making those off-based statements even though I did not ask for an apology in my letter.

Lack of Diversity

More often than what we may realize is the fact that a lack of consideration and/ or appreciation for diversity precipitates numerous problems for people in our society. As example, while living in Huntington, West Virginia several years ago, it did not take very long for our Sunday school class to recognize that our regular appointed teacher was a staunch conservative. He was not bashful in expressing his views that he strongly felt that a man was always considered the head of the household ... whether one was present or not. Upon his absence on certain Sundays, he made sure that a man was designated as the substitute teacher. One Sunday, "equal rights" in the workplace became a topic of discussion in the class. The teacher stated that he agreed with equal rights on the job for everyone as long as women stayed in their place. A woman placed in a position whereby she would supervise men presented a challenge for the teacher. He further stated that his wife was a strong willed person but she knew her proper place at home, work and at the church. Although no one challenged the teacher that day in the class regarding his lack of consideration and appreciation for diversity, actions were later put in motion to expose him. During the next week, several members of the class met with the church pastor and informed him that something needed to be done about the Sunday school teacher's behavior. They asked that the pastor either effect a change in the teacher's expressed views or replace him with someone else. We got a new teacher.

One day as I was making walk-through rounds in our Dietetic Service at the medical center in Alabama, a female supervisor called me aside and stated, "I cannot bring myself together to be able to work with white people." I quietly told her that she needed to go to our Human Resources Service as soon as possible to resign. She asked why should she resign if she did not like white folks. I informed her that by signing resignation documents, it would allow her to leave the organization and not have to worry about working with anybody. She never went to Human Resources to sign resignation documents but I am certain the point was well taken as it relates to diversity and being able to work with others from various races and backgrounds.

The deficit in nature of consideration for diversity in most cases will cause a need for an apology. An example is the case involving former National Basketball Association (NBA) All-Star basketball player Tim Hardaway. While appearing on a Miami radio talk show in February 2007, Mr. Hardaway was asked how he would interact with a gay teammate. The question was probably asked because just a week before the interview, it was announced that Mr. John Amaechi became the first former NBA player to say he was gay. Mr. Hardaway response to the question was somewhat surprising since he represented the league. He said, "First of all, I wouldn't want him on my team. And second of all, if he was on my team, I would, you know, really distance myself from him because, uh, I don't think that is right. I don't think he should be in the locker room while we are in the locker room." When the show host informed Mr. Hardaway that his comments were "flatly homophobic" and "bigotry," Mr. Hardaway statements made things even worse. He continued, "You know, I hate gay people, so I let it be known. I don't like gay people and I don't like to be around gay people. I'm homophobic. I don't like it. It shouldn't be in the world or in the United States."

Mr. Hardaway apologized for the comments he made on the radio talk show. He said, "As an African-American, I know all too well the negative thoughts and feelings hatred and bigotry cause. I regret and apologize for the statements that I made that have certainly caused the same kinds of feelings and reactions. I especially apologize to my fans, friends and family in Miami and Chicago. I am committed to examining my feelings and will recognize, appreciate and respect the differences among people in our society. I regret any embarrassment I have caused the league on the eve of one of their greatest annual events."

The apology appeared to be genuine and reflected all of the appropriate elements to constitute one. However, it is very difficult to determine whether the apology will help Mr. Hardaway's image in the future and embarrassments to the radio station and the NBA. He probably will not be given another opportunity to represent the NBA. Immediately following reports of the broadcast, the commissioner of the NBA, Mr. David Stern, banned Mr. Hardaway from participating in the upcoming NBA's All-Star basketball game for making the anti-gay remarks. Mr. Hardaway was already in Las Vegas where the game was to be played and had scheduled a series of public appearances on behalf of the league. Mr. Stern stated that, "We removed him from representing us because we didn't think his comments were consistent with having anything to do with us. This issue overall has fascinated America. This is a country that needs to talk about this issue, and not surprisingly, they use sports as a catalyst to begin the dialogue."

I agree with a part of one of the statements made by the commissioner when he said, "This is a country that needs to talk about this issue ..." However, I disagree with his insinuation that sports (NBA or NFL) is being used as a springboard to address diversity in our country, as the latter part of his statement was, "and not surprisingly, they use sports as a catalyst to begin the dialogue." Probably unintentionally, but the commissioner identified the major underlining challenge we have with diversity in our nation. No one, including our large organizations, wants to acknowledge ownership and responsibility for making diversity effective. Most people feel that it is the other person's responsibility to effectuate it. The need goes far beyond having respect and appreciation for gay people, but primarily for having recognition for diversity from a practical perspective. If one were to thoroughly review the NBA's policy files, it is doubtful that a single policy directive would be found relating to diversity in the league with the exception of the newly established dress code. But diversity does exist beyond the off-the-court dress code. Take a look at the various hairstyles and sneakers being displayed in the NBA today.

While most members of some organizations such as the NBA accept diversity as an element of doing business, there are others whose members consider this quality or state of affairs as a cardinal sin. Undoubtedly, some members of the Episcopal Church are not receptive to diversity. The Episcopal Church approved a gay bishop in 2003 and elected a female bishop in 2006. Presiding Bishop Katharine Jefferts Schori announced in 2006 that she supports blessing gay unions. However, following this announcement, several churches have seceded from the Episcopal Church to align with the Archbishop of Nigeria. It may very well be a situation where some say, "You are damned if you do and damned if you don't."

The word diversity has numerous definitions. Webster's New World Dictionary defines diversity as quality, state, fact, or instance of being difference. The dictionary also uses the words dissimilarity and variety to describe diversity. For the purpose of this book, we will use my layman's definition for diversity: "A state of recognition that there are differences in the people we interact with in our society. It emphasizes the application of individual differences to build effective groups, organizations and the nation as a whole. Individual differences relate to race, ethnicity, gender, sexual orientation, age, physical capabilities, nationality, professional discipline, cultural heritage and other unique attributes."

Another example where lack of consideration and/or appreciation for diversity was very painful is the case involving radio talk show host Don Imus. There was an enormous outcry and demand that Mr. Imus of MSNBC be fired after he referred to the Rutgers women's basketball players as "nappy-headed hos" on April 4, 2007. The Don Imus radio talk show is owned by CBS and televised by MSNBC network. The statements were made as Mr. Imus was speaking with producer Bernard McGuirk about the NCAA women's national title game between Rutgers and Tennessee. Mr. McGuirk referred to the mostly black (8) Rutgers players as "some hardcore hos." Mr. Imus stated, "That's some nappy-headed hos there, I'm going to tell you that." It was reported on the next day after the above comments were made that Mr. Imus downplayed his statements by saying it was "some idiot comment meant to be amusing." A Rutgers spokesperson issued a statement saying, we agree with Mr. Imus that this was, in his own words, an 'idiot comment.'"

Once the furor over the comments about the Rutgers female basketball players had gotten started, it seems that nothing could be done to avert its attention. On Friday, April 6, the storm of criticisms over the comments got worse by more and more people joining in on the call for more apologies and termination of Mr. Imus.

Mr. Imus' apology on April 6 contained all of the elements that constituted a genuine apology except one. He said that he wanted to "apologize for an insensitive and ill-conceived remark we made the other morning referring to the Rutgers women's basketball team. It was completely inappropriate, and we can understand why people were offended. Our characterization was thoughtless and stupid, and we are sorry." Mr. Imus did not indicate at that time he would not make similar insulting statements about a group again.

On Tuesday, April 10, it was announced that MSNBC and CBC Radio had suspended Don Imus for two weeks for making the comments about the Rutgers female basketball players. NBC officials stated that Mr. Imus' "Abhorrent comments" left them little choice but to suspend him, but that they believe his pledge to "change the discourse" on his show. Another contributory reason that can be speculated as a factor for the suspension is that Mr. Imus has had a long history of making insulting remarks about people on his radio show. Records show that he or his staff has been criticized for going too far on several occasions on his shows, including an impersonation of poet Maya Angelou; called Colin Powell a "weasel,'" called New Mexico Governor Bill Richardson a "fat sissy;" referred to Senator Ben Nighthorse Campbell of Colorado, an American Indian, as "the guy from 'F Troop;'" and called the New York Knicks basketball players a group of "chest-thumping pimps." Mr. Imus indicated that the punishment was appropriate but stressed, "I am not a racist."

Leaders representing blacks, including the Rev. Al Sharpton had asked that Mr. Imus be fired. Rev. Sharpton also stated that he was going to complain to the Federal Communication Commission about the comments. The Rev. Jesse Jackson with a group of 50 protesters marched outside NBC offices in Chicago on April 9 and also said that the two-week suspension was not enough. Mr. James E. Harris, president of the New Jersey chapter of the National Association for the Advancement of Colored People (NAACP), demanded on April 9 that Mr. Imus "resign or be terminated immediately." The Detroit branch of the NAACP also asked that Mr. Imus be fired. But there were other critics who felt that Mr. Imus had gone too far in his ill characterization of the players. The media networks that air the show expressed concerns about the comments. Ms. Allison Gollust, spokeswoman for MSNBC, said the network considered Imus' comments "deplorable." Ms. Karen Mateo, spokeswoman for CBC Radio, said the company was "disappointed" in Mr. Imus' actions and characterized his comments as "completely inappropriate." In a joint statement, NCAA president Myles Brand and Rutgers president Richard McCormick said, "It is unconscionable that anyone would use the airways to utter such disregard for the dignity of human beings who have accomplished much and deserve great credit." Mr. Bryan Monroe, president of the National Association of Black Journalists, stated that, "What he said has deeply hurt too many people, black and white, male and female. His so-called apology comes two days after the fact, and it is too little, too late." The National Organization for Women also asked that Mr. Imus be fired for making the comments about the women basketball players.

Also on Tuesday, April 10, the Rutgers female basketball players held a news conference where they talked about the comments Mr. Imus made about them. They presented a very good case for themselves … that they were not "hos." Webster's New World Dictionary defines "hos" as, "An exclamation of pleasure, surprise, derision, etc. An exclamation to attract attention: sometimes used after a destination or direction." The public learned from their presentations and responses that these young women had done well in the classrooms and continued to excel in that area while performing exceptional on the basketball court. More significance was the fact that a majority of them had promising futures ahead of them in professional areas such as medicine, education and musical entertainment.

On April 11, it was announced that several of the sponsors of the Imus' radio and TV talk show had withdrawn their advertisements from the program. The firestorm continued as politicians and others intervened and demanded that Mr. Imus be fired. Reports indicated that on the same day, several angry NBC News employees, many of them black, met with news division president Steve Capus and informed him that they felt the two-week suspension for Mr. Imus was not sufficient punishment. Consequently, Mr. Capus decided to terminate Mr. Imus' show on MSNBC. Mr. Capus stated that Mr. Imus' comments had "touched a nerve" within the organization and they questioned themselves as to "when is enough going to be enough?" He said, "This was the only action we could take." Some experts had previously indicated that termination action would never happen because of the enormous amount of money that was generated from the program through advertisement. As example, it was reported that advertisers spent approximately $11.3 million in 2006 on the show. Sponsors paid MSNBC an additional $8.4 million during the same period for advertisement spots on the show. CBS obtained more than $14 million each year through advertising on the radio station (WFAN) show program.

After MSNBC had announced that they were terminating Mr. Imus from their daily morning telecast, pressure begin to escalate that CBS Radio should follow MSNBC's lead. Critics strongly advocated that Mr. Imus must be fired by CBS in order for the network to maintain a respectable image. On Thursday, April 12, CBS announced that they had dropped the Don Imus radio talk show, essentially firing him for making racist remarks about the Rutgers women's basketball team. Mr. Imus met with the team and coaches for approximately three hours the night following the announcement that he was fired. The team head coach, Ms. C. Vivian Stringer later announced that the team players had forgiven Mr. Imus for the remarks.

Certain aspects of the furor are somewhat confusing. The first response from critics about the comments Mr. Imus made seems to indicate that all he needed to do to amend the situation was for him to offer a genuine apology. The Rev. Al Sharpton asked that Mr. Imus be fired but gave him a chance to apologize and state his case for making the comments on the Reverend's radio talk show. Mr. Bryan Monroe, president of the National Association of Black Journalists (NABJ) said both Imus and McGuirk should be fired unless they issued more thorough apologies.

Mr. Imus complied with Rev. Sharpton's request. He appeared on the radio show and offered another apology. Mr. Imus further stated that, "Here's what I've learned: that you can't make fun of everybody, because some people don't deserve it. And because the climate on this program has been what it's been for 30 years doesn't mean that it has to be that way for the next five years or whatever because that has to change, and I understand that." On his own show Tuesday morning, April 10, Imus said, "What I did was make a stupid, idiotic mistake in a comedy context." He said his staff had tried to set up a meeting with Rutgers players and their families so he could apologize to them.

The confusion over the furor relates to the fact that Mr. Imus apologized as requested, was suspended and then terminated by both MSNBC and CBS for making the ill-conceived comments. More perplexing in the case is that some critics wanted an apology, some wanted a termination and still others wanted both. Reports did not disclose that anyone had asked for a suspension. However, the question remains: Will the two actions taken make a difference in how the affected people will feel about Mr. Imus in the future? The confusion and aftermath over the furor certainly confirm my theory that one should never ask or demand an apology. All that was needed in the situation was a statement of rejection of the comments Mr. Imus made. Afterward, the onus of taking proper actions against Mr. Imus would have been the responsibility of the network owners and sponsors of the program.

Opinion polls were taken during the height of the furor and a number of people indicated that they felt the statements made by Mr. Imus caused no harm to anyone and some even got a big laugh from the remarks. The people who thought the statements were funny and not offensive are just as guilty as Mr. Imus and his producer, Mr. McGuirk. Racial and sexual comments are never funny in the hearts of the offended. I was advised many years ago that the best way to stay out of trouble in regard to racial and sexual jokes or statements is to never engage in them at all … even when it is about your own race or sex.

But what makes the situation more confusing, disgusting and even nauseating is the fact that the same words used by Mr. Imus on his radio program are used every day by rap groups, hip hop artists and others, especially in our black communities without any fanfare or objection. In fact, these groups are given prestigious awards each year for the songs and/or rap music they present with the use of these words. What Don Imus said was wrong and insulting to many people. However, it is more insulting and disgusting when blacks use the same words about themselves and nobody questions it. Don Imus learned those words by listening to black people who used them in their rap songs. If their survival were dependent upon my purchasing of their records, they would have defunct many, many years ago! If people do not buy the records, the rap artists will not exist or they will have to clean up their lyrics. I strongly agree with The Reverend Roosevelt Wright, Jr., editor for the Monroe Free Press newspaper when he said, "We do not have exclusive rights at self-degradation. If we don't want others to refer to us as 'niggas, nappy heads, bitches, and hos' then let's clean up our own act before we get so self righteous that we want others fired for saying what we say about ourselves."

A lack of consideration and/or appreciation for diversity shows up in our society in other various forms. Some people feel that it is "moral correct" to force their religious, moral values, or beliefs on others. This contention was reflected in another request for advise by a concerned person from Dear Abby. The person of concern wrote, "Is it appropriate ('Carrie' is a widow and 'Jake' is divorced) to wear wedding bands on the ring fingers of their left hands? They say they are 'married in their hearts' and cannot marry legally for financial reasons. My husband and I feel that the wearing of wedding bands without following the rules of marriage (I.e., a ceremony conducted by a person licensed to marry and the receiving of a legal document) diminishes the sanctity and authenticity of our own wedding bands and those of all others who are legally married." Abby's response was, "Couples who find themselves in the situation of the couple you have described sometime discuss it with their clergyperson and exchange vows so they can be 'married in the eyes of God.' Because Carrie and Jake's marital situation bothers you so much, why don't you mention this to them? After that, however, I would urge you to devote your attention to your own marriage, because how others choose to conduct their lives is no reflection on the sanctity and authenticity of your wedding bands—and frankly, it's none of your business." Without questions or further explanations, the last sentence of the response put the supposed concern in its proper perspective.

How does an organization launch a diversity initiative? There are consultants and other experts available in this area that can provide invaluable insight on the implementation of a diversity initiative. All organizations, large and small should have an idea of the composition of its workforce and other unique attributes that make them operate the way they do. If employed, the consultants' first action probably would be a collection of data relating to demographic profile, managerial and non-managerial workforce, promotions and other employee performance indicators. The consultants will probably conduct an employees' survey to measure their perceptions, attitudes and other opinions about the organization. Undoubtedly, diversity training would be provided to educate the entire workforce in the organization on the value of recognition and appreciation of an effective diversity ongoing initiative.

Etiquette and Apology

An adequate discussion on the nature of apologies cannot be completed without mentioning etiquette. Etiquette is defined by Webster's New World Dictionary as, the forms, manners, and ceremonies established by convention as acceptable or required in social relations, in a profession, or in official life. Consequently, when a person apologizes to another as a result of an insult or whatever, the reaction is considered proper etiquette. Author Harriette Cole in her book, "How to Be Contemporary Etiquette for African Americans" stated that, "Etiquette is more than knowing which fork to use. Good manners are the rules that let us find our way in today's world of lifestyles, customs and relationships. Anyone who doesn't know these rules is living and working at a real disadvantage. It does not matter how smart or educated or even how rich you are ... bad manners will hold you back."

Apologizing for hurting, insulting or causing any other harm to another person is easy for some people but is very difficult for others. Some people are naturally at ease in relating to others and do not have to have formal training. However, most people who want to be successful on the job, at social events and in general at apologizing should augment their knowledge of it with structured lessons in communication and interpersonal skills. We can also learn a great deal on the subject by reading information of the subject and observing others. In almost all encounters, we tend to gravitate toward our own strength and we do not like to be asked to do something that makes us feel uneasy. Some social experts say on an average, men have a more difficult time apologizing than women. Why? It is said that women do not feel as vulnerable as men. Results from certain studies showed that most men would not admit they were wrong in a disagreement, especially if the other party was a woman. For some reason, maybe due to high self-esteem, men feel an apology would weaken their power position with people. On the other hand, it has been said that women are more apt to offer an apology when one is needed as well as when one is probably not needed. Women are labeled to take this approach primarily because they are known to be habitual "talkers." Having this label is not all bad since it has been shown that an apologetic manner will relieve tensions and ameliorate bad feelings in tenuous situations. The act of openly discussing an issue or problem is considered a much better approach than keeping the matter to yourself in most instances.

In another book on etiquette, "Essential Manners for Men," Peter Post, stated that, "the art of etiquette really comes down to being thoughtful of the other people you encounter in your everyday life. We all tend to associate `proper behavior` with formal social events, but true etiquette involves behaving with respect and consideration for others in everything that you do, from attending a high-society soiree to simply hanging out around the house."

Certain statements and/or actions made by people, as the "old folks" would say, are bound to precipitate resentment or controversy. As example, when former heavyweight boxing champion, Mike Tyson bit off part of one of Evander Holyfield's ear in June 1997, there was no question the act would be controversial. After the incident, boxing commissions considered banning Tyson from the sports for life. Although Tyson made statements that he called an apology for his actions, many sports fans lost respect for him as an individual and/or boxer.

Following the incident of biting Holyfield, Tyson stated that he was seeking psychological help. Tyson has been involved in other incidents where he has acted a little off-centered. According to a newspaper article, while Tyson was riding in a car with his wife on a Maryland expressway an accident occurred in which they were involved. Tyson's wife had to make a sudden stop because the car ahead of her made an unexpected stop. However, Tyson's wife hit the car in front of her from behind and the car behind them hit the Tysons' car. Obviously, Mr. Tyson was not thoughtful of others. Instead, he appears to have a problem of blaming others whenever anything goes wrong. This also means that he always believe his perceptions of a situation are right. And even worse, he believes that he should be the one to resolve the problem and not law officials. It was reported that Mike Tyson hit the driver of the car in front of them for stopping too quickly and he also hit the driver of the car behind them for rear-ending their car. An apology was not offered.

In Monroe, LA in December 2006, what was supposed to have been a fundraiser for the Monroe Chamber of Commerce by sponsoring a dinner affair with the state Governor, Kathleen Blanco, turned into a big embarrassment. The embarrassment came about when the only bid for the dinner was $1. The President of the Monroe Chamber of Commerce called the Governor and apologized for the affront. Monroe banker, Malcolm Maddox, who made the $1 bid, also apologized and later wrote a check donation for $1000. The governor said she was not offended by the action and/or lack of respect.

> Although apologies were offered and the governor was commended for her support and responsiveness to the chamber and the area at large, damage had been done. It was reported by the local newspaper, The News-Star, that the $1 dinner bid had caught the attention of national media. The News-Star editorial board put the incident in proper perspective with the following article, "Faux Pas Leaves Area Red-Faced, We often decry the lack of propriety demonstrated by young people today. But local business leader's recent public affront to our state's governor demonstrates that well-heeled adults don't always get it either. Last week local bank president Malcolm Maddox made a $1 winning bid on a dinner with Gov. Kathleen Blanco at the Monroe Chamber of Commerce's annual auction. Maddox has not returned calls from The News-Star, so we can only surmise the intent of his actions. Our society has come to embrace a difference of political opinions as an excuse to wink at bad manners. Well, it is not. Gov. Kathleen Blanco's response to the insult was generous. Rather than seize the moment for political gain, the governor graciously deflected the insult—as a well-mannered person would do. Unlike a monarchial system of government, our democratically elected leaders come from our midst. Perhaps this is why debasing remarks that would be treason against a monarch often fail to give us pause. We have it wrong. The position of governor—regardless of politics—is due respect. This governor certainly has our respect. The $1000 check Maddox subsequently handed over to the chamber was appropriate, but it does not excuse the apparent slight. In this case, we offer a simple apology for the embarrassment and disrespect—as this story has spread nationwide—that emanated, misguidedly, from our region."

It appears that the key behavior relative to proper etiquette is found in "being thoughtful and/or consideration of others." This probably will give rise to the fact that if proper etiquette had been employed upfront, there would not be a need for an apology. Being inconsiderate and being disrespectful are very much the same. In respecting others you should always give people the benefit of the doubt. A person will never be sorry for showing compassion. When we treat other people with proper respect, their feelings will resonate and rub-off on others. It is safe to conclude that some statements and actions are best when they are never said or done.

Children seem to have a better feel than some grown-ups about when to offer an apology. Most of them learn this behavior at home. 4-year old Blake decided to take two of his Power Rangers toys with him into the dentist office to play with while waiting for his sister who was being seen by the dentist. When he arrived in the office he discovered that the office had toys for children to play with in a playroom. As he put his Power Rangers aside to play with some of the office toys a little girl came in and grabbed the Power Rangers to play with. Upon noticing this, Blake stated, "Those are my Power Rangers." The little girl responded, "I am sorry. I don't want to take your toys. I will play with some of the other toys over there."

Ahmani always took her lunch to school and placed it in an assigned area in the classroom. One day when she went to retrieve her lunch to eat it, she discovered that someone had taken it, leaving only the bread trimming in the bag. Ahmani's little friend said, "Ahmani, I am sorry that someone stole your lunch. I will be glad to share my lunch with you." It is gratifying to observe that Ahmani's friend apologized for somebody else devilishness.

An Apology Was Expected ...
But One Was Not Offered

In some instances an apology is not warranted? Singer, Britney Spears' fans and others who like to watch her in public life disapproved of Spears' flashing her apparent lack of underwear to the paparazzi in December 2006. Her fans and other watchers were unhappy by the fact that as she celebrated her 25th birthday on nights out with party girls Paris Hilton and Lindsay Lohan, photographers caught what some thought were uncensored, R-rated crotch shots that were placed on the Internet. Spears did not offer an apology for her actions. Instead, she put her actions in proper perspectives by saying, "It been so long since I've been out on the town with friends. It's also been 2 years since I've even celebrated my birthday. Every move I make at this point has been magnified more than I expected, and I probably did take my newfound freedom (after filing for divorce) a little too far. Anyway, thank God for Victoria's Secret's new underwear line! I look forward to a new year, new music and a new me." There was not a need for Ms. Spears to apologize for something she wanted to do and was compelled to do so.

Leonard Pitts, columnist for the Miami Herald, was prompted to write in one of his February 2007 articles that he was not going to apologize for making a statement that, "Children need fathers." The article, "No apologies: Children need fathers," was written in response to an e-mail Mr. Pitts said he received informing him that he was an "anti-gay bigot." The person who sent the e-mail message was apparently upset with the statements Mr. Pitts made in a column written about Ms. Mary Cheney, who is a lesbian, was pregnant at the time, and is the daughter of Vice-President Dick Cheney. It was considered a coincident that Mr. Pitts was slated to receive an honorary award from Parents & Friends of Lesbians & Gays (PFLAG) within a few weeks of getting the e-mail. Since parenting and adoption of children are now highly charged emotion issues in our society, Mr. Pitts' response will be shown here in its entirety. He wrote, "I thought it a bad idea for Cheney and her life mate, Heather Poe, to have a baby, and I noted that this is an opinion I share with Dr. James Dobson of Focus on the Family fame. Which caused a few folks to fire off scandalized notes wondering how I function without benefit of a brain. Or a heart.

I suppose you can't blame them for going nuclear at an expression of solidarity with Dobson, who is not known for his enlightened attitude toward gays. For the record, had he couched his objection in terms of antipathy toward gays, I'd have happily torn him a new orifice. But he did not. What he said was something I have often said myself: children need fathers.

That argument, for me, at least, is not about sexual orientation. My objection to Cheney and Poe is precisely the same one I have to heterosexual single women who decide to conceive children without benefit of a stable and involved father. I believe that our slide toward a fatherless society, a society where the male parent is considered optional, irrelevant or interchangeable, is toxic for our children.

That concern is buttressed by a growing body of research—UC Santa Barbara, 1996, University of Pennsylvania, 1997, Princeton University and the University of Pennsylvania, 1998, London School of Economics and Princeton University, 2002—which tells us the child raised without his or her biological father is significantly more likely to live in poverty, do poorly in school, drop out altogether, become a teen parent, exhibit behavioral problems, smoke, drink, use drugs, or wind up in jail. So dad's involvement would seem vital to a child's well-being.

And in reading those e-mails, I was repeatedly struck by the blithe way people disregarded that fact, by how eagerly they assured me fathers bring nothing to the table that cannot be replaced by an uncle, a coach, a family friend or other "father figure." As one woman put it: 'To say that chromosomes or genitalia dictate the chances of happiness or success … for a family really makes no sense.'

Actually, what makes no sense is to pretend that you can remove a father from a child's life and have the child not notice. I mean, can you imagine anyone daring to make the argument that children lose nothing if their mother abandons them, that the emotional support, nurturing and unqualified love she brings to the home can be readily replaced by the friendly lady down the street? Of course not.

That some of us so airily make that exact argument about fathers speaks volumes about our lack of respect for—and understanding of—fatherhood itself. I have nothing against father figures. I had one. I am one. But a father figure is not a father.

I also have nothing against gay adoptive parents or mothers left single by tragedy, divorce or abandonment. I admire them. But as 16 percent of white kids and a whopping 51 percent of black ones grow up father free, facing all the difficulties that portends, I definitely have something against the idea, whether advanced by straight women or lesbians, that father is unnecessary, that so long as there's some uncle around to show a boy how to hit the mark in the toilet, everything is hunky dory.

A woman has the right to use her body as she sees fit. I don't argue that. But it seems to me her child has a few rights, too."

Many true stories have been told about the single parent, especially those on the part of the mother. There is another coincident in relation to this article ... I have always had the same feelings.

It is gravely unfortunate how some people spend a half of a lifetime grieving over the fact that they did not get an apology from an offender. The offended person may have suffered due to circumstances thought to be unjust to him or her. The offending person may have been a relative, such as a father who was considered to be a deadbeat and inconsiderate. This behavior is illustrated in a "Dear Abby" request for help published on December 22, 2006. The person wrote, "Dear Abby: My parents split when I was 3 and divorced when I was 6. I am now 28. Mama remarried when I was 7 to a man I consider to be my dad. My biological father, "Kevin," lived in the same town we did until I was 11, when we moved. (My father was in the military) Communications and visits were rare before we moved and have been nearly nonexistent ever since. Kevin never paid child support and only occasionally remembered birthdays when I was young. He called once a few years ago. The entire conversation was centered on his making excuses about why he was never around and never supported us. In the end, he blamed Mama for it. He never once apologized for being a deadbeat dad or his lack of interest in my life. Kevin called again a few months ago. I was civil to him although I didn't offer much in the way of conversation. He said he and his wife had prepared their wills and that I was named in his. I simply said, "OK" and didn't ask any questions. Kevin has called a couple of times since, but I have no motivation to return his calls. This week I got a birthday card from him in the mail—two weeks late, of course. It contained a check for a small amount of money. I honestly did not feel any loss for not having Kevin in my life because I was blessed with a loving, caring male parent. Sharing DNA does not constitute being a father in my book. But I think he at least owes me an apology or some kind of admission of wrongdoing (or lack of doing) if he expects me to be civil and communicate with him. Should I return the check? Should I cash it, and write a letter thanking him for remembering my birthday, albeit late? Or should I tell him I am not willing to talk to him until he's willing to offer me an apology?" Abby informed the distraught daughter, "For someone who "honestly did not feel any loss for not having him in (your) life," you appear to be genuinely steamed at your birth father. The time has come to be honest with yourself about your feelings of anger, disappointment and abandonment—and tell him honestly how you feel. Then hear him out. You may learn that your mother made it diffi-cult for your father to see you—and the move reinforced it. He may also have had financial problems that made monetary support difficult. Only he can give you the details that, in my opinion, you sorely need to hear. It is clear your father is now trying to make amend, even if it's not in the form of an apology." The request and response indicated that there is no substitute for communications between the offender and the offended parties when an opportunity exists for one.

Every active person on earth has intentionally and/or unintentionally caused harm to another person or group of persons whether they have recognized it or not. Every sound minded person has some degree of compassion and empathy in his or her heart. If a person refuse to apologize after it has been made known that he or she has hurt and/or humiliated another person, the right thing to do is not to ask or demand an apology. Instead of asking for an apology it is suggested that the offended person forgive the offender for his or her action. We can never over-emphasize forgiveness or its value in moving on with our lives. A. Battista was quoted as saying, "One of the most lasting pleasures you can experience is the feeling that comes over you when you genuinely forgive an enemy ... whether he knows about it or not." By not receiving an apology is not the end of the world no matter how severe the insult or inconsideration may feel. Move on with your life is the right thing to do. There are more important things in life beside an apology. While serving as medical center director in VA, one day a veteran came to my office to complain about a statement one of our doctors made to him while he was being examined. The veteran stated that after he had described all of his health problems to the doctor, the doctor promptly said, "You think you have problems. Wait until you hear about my problems!" The veteran was offended and very upset by the doctor's remarks. I made an attempt to apologize on behalf of the doctor but it was to no avail. The veteran wanted a personal apology from the offending doctor. After discussing the issue with the doctor, arrangements were made for the veteran to report for a visit where the doctor made an apology. The doctor told the veteran that he was very sorry that he made the statements and regretted that the statements were hurtful to him. The doctor also stated that he never should have made the offending statements and he would have felt the same way if his private physician had made similar statements to him. The following day I received a memorandum from the doctor indicating that he had met with the veteran and apologized. Approximately two months later I saw the same veteran at a veteran's organization conference. The veteran informed me that he still had not received an apology from the doctor. After informing the veteran that I had received a note from the doctor showing a date in which an apology was made and what had been said, he admitted one had been made and asked to be forgiven for bring the subject up again.

Making an attempt to apologize can be dangerous, even deadly in some cases. During the early fall of 2006, Grambling State University's quarterback Brandon Landers and his brother Frank were attending a high school football game when a fight broke out near where they were sitting in the stands. Frank intervened to break up the altercation. After the game, Frank sensed that one of the parties in the altercation was still angry. Consequently, he asked his brother, Brandon, to drive him over to the young man's house since he knew him personally and where he lived. Upon arriving at the man's house, Frank discovered that the man was even angrier. In an attempt to apologize and ameliorate the confrontation, Frank was shot and later died at a local medical center.

On another hand, in some instances an apology should have been offered following what appeared to be a case where harm was done but the gesture was not made. An 11-year old boy's family in Garden City, N.Y. sued Taco Bell, claiming negligence by the restaurant chain caused the child to fall ill to E. coli amid an outbreak that had sickened nearly four dozen other people. The boy became ill after eating three tacos with cheese and lettuce on November 24, 2006. He was hospitalized four days later and released from the hospital a day after admission. Taco Bell employees removed scallions from all 5,800 of its restaurants after preliminary tests linked them to the bacteria. State and federal officials initiated an investigation on the outbreak after the incident received media attentions. The Taco Bell chain should have immediately offered an apology to all parties who may have been harmed by the outbreak. Instead, a Taco Bell spokeswoman said the company had no immediate comment on the lawsuit. "In an abundance of caution, we've decided to pull all green onions from our restaurants until we know conclusively whether they are the cause of the E. coli outbreak," said Greg Creed, president of Taco Bell. As far as could be determined, there were no further comments made by the company to express regret for the outbreak.

During the 2004 Super Bowl half-time performance, Janet Jackson allowed co-performer Justin Timberlake to expose her breast. Neither Ms Jackson nor Mr. Timberlake apologized for the intentional antics although they called it an accident. Sometimes accidents can get us in a lot of trouble! Ms. Jackson had been previously invited to participate in the Grammy Awards program the following week but she canceled. She also withdrew from an ABC biotic about singer Lena Horne. A Jackson spokeswoman told Variety Magazine that Ms. Horne was displeased by Ms. Jackson's Super Bowl half-time antics and wanted ABC to pull Ms. Jackson off the movie. The network refused, but Ms. Jackson and the producers quit anyway. It was later said that Ms. Jackson's public image took a temporary nose-dive, whereas Mr. Timberlake's image stayed relatively unchanged.

Another situation where an apology was expected immediately after an incident but was not given, involved the local city of Monroe Police Department in December 2006. A law enforcement officer was fired after he accused the Chief Police of illegally audio taping him while he worked at the police station. After the officer discovered the cameras and microphones, he reported the crime to the local Sheriff and to the State Police. The State Attorney General office presented its investigation results to a grand jury for appropriate actions. Several people testified before the grand jury. However, just before the officer was to testify, a secret meeting was held whereby a deal was made for the officer. He was allowed to drop charges against the Chief Police, return to work, be protected from the Chief and given an opportunity to retire in three years. A transcript of the deal involving the officer, the Chief Police, their attorneys, the city attorney and the State attorney revealed that all parties in the meeting had agreed to confidentiality of the terms of the deal. The day before copies of the transcript were obtained the Chief Police told the media that there was no connection between the dismissal of the grand jury complaint and the officer's rehiring. But a document was signed and notarized the very same day restoring the officer to employment with the department for exchange for dropping his criminal complaint against the Chief Police. None of the parties (Mayor, Chief Police, State Attorney General, or attorney for the city) who participated in the case offered an apology to the citizens (taxpayers) of the area for not taking necessary criminal actions or for misusing funds.

Still another example can be found in the case involving a 98-year old great grandmother. It was reported in a local newspaper on December 23, 2006 that a 98-year old woman was sent a water bill by the city of Monroe for $2,594.82. When the great granddaughter who usually pays the bills for her great grandmother noticed the unusually high billing for water, she presented it to the city's water department for resolution because she was certain it was an error. The great granddaughter even visited the mayor's office in her attempt to resolve the issue. The mayor's secretary stated that the mayor had a full schedule, as usual and she was not seen there. After the granddaughter complained to several other city officials about the unusual high bill, the city agreed to read the water meter again and reported that the consumption reading was correct. The granddaughter was told that the bill ($2,594.82) had to be paid. After she continued to complain that there was no way possible the great grandmother could have used such large amount of water, the meter was read again. And again, the water department officials stated that the reading was correct. The great granddaughter did not relinquish her claim that the billing was excessive and indicated that her great grandmother used water only for bathing (three times a week) bathroom needs and drinking. The great grandmother did not cook as the great granddaughter performed that task for her. At the end of the day a city official called and offered to reduce the bill to $100. The great granddaughter refused to pay the $100 because the highest most recent bill was for only $28. Finally, the city provided her with a new bill for $14.16. There was no adjustment made on the meter reading but the consumption amount was removed. The great granddaughter stated that the city did not provide an explanation as to how they arrived at the $14.16 new charge. The great granddaughter stated, "My grandmother is 98 years old. If she had seen this bill she would have died. The city never apologized for the error or assumed any responsibility for it."

Politics is probably the worse area where an apology is procrastinated or avoided altogether. It appears that most politicians feel that they are immune from apologizing. Former Congressman Mark Foley from Florida apologized to his constituents only after he had been exposed and advised to so. U.S. Representative William Jefferson of Louisiana has never offered an apology for the investigation into the alleged bribery charges nor an explanation why $90,000 in marked bills were found in his home freezer. The Congressman was under investigation the entire two years of his last term in office. He denied any wrongdoings relative to the allegations and was reelected to office in December 2006. Congressman Jefferson stated after the election that he was glad to be back in Congress to serve the citizens of his District in New Orleans.

There has been a mass calling for President George W. Bush to apologize to American citizens for engagement in the Iraq war. Countless number of journalists, domestic "think-tank" groups and others are now suggesting that the President should say, "I am very sorry that we (U.S.) went into Iraq." Instead of continuing to say, "We must stay the course." An engagement of the country in war by a president will almost always create strong oppositions from various sources. However, when President Bush ordered an invasion of Afghanistan to rid the country of Osama bin Laden and the Taliban, there was little fanfare about the ordeal even through Osama bin Laden slipped away and is still believed to have great influence on terrorism.

The war in Iraq is a different story because there have been different outcomes. In 2003, President Bush had the U.S. military to lead a coalition of forces to invade Iraq and depose Saddam Hussein. The primary reason for this action was due to evidence that the country under the direction of Saddam Hussein was concealing weapons of mass destruction. The offensive action also was advanced as a means toward the war on terrorism.

The Iraq war plans have not worked out as they were developed. Some critics have said that there were never any plans. Saddam Hussein was captured, removed from office and executed in December 2006. Weapons of mass destruction were not found in Iraq after considerable efforts were made searching for them. The weapons of mass destruction blunder was blamed on faulty intelligent work of the Central Intelligence Agency (CIA). The president feels that continuation of the Iraq war is fully justified and promising initiative to control terrorism and implant democracy. But as the war has now gone pass three years, many people as reflected in various opinion polls, feel that it was a thoughtless blunder by the president and his administration where fighting and lost of lives have been a false pursuit of non-existent weapons of mass destruction and imaginary links to the September 11, 2001 attacks.

The American people's opinions about the war in Iraq have showed up in various forms. Protests in the form of picketing and sit-ins began after the first year of engagement. In March 2006, an opinion poll on the war showed 57% of those surveyed said the Iraq war was a mistake. Support for the war in Iraq has diminished primarily because of certain hard facts. In January 2007, the Associated Press counted more than 3,000 members of the U.S. military had died since the beginning of the war in March 2003. The report also showed more than 10,000 other U.S. casualties with several thousand considered as highly critical. The cost of the war in Iraq to U.S. taxpayers has been reported to be eight billion dollars a month.

On December 6, 2006, a bipartisan Iraq Study Group reported that the president's policy in Iraq was not working. The group's assessment called for an urgent need for a diplomatic attempt to stabilize the country and allow withdrawal of most U.S. combat troops by early 2008. In all, the report offered 79 recommendations, including a need for the president to put aside misgivings and engage Syria, Iran and the leaders of insurgent forces in negotiations on the country's future.

On January 10, 2007, President Bush held a news conference to disclose his new strategy for Iraq to American people. The new strategy called for a temporary U.S. combat troops build up around Baghdad and a mandate that the Iraq government will take charge of security for the country. Prior to the president's address, a U S Today/Gallows poll showed that 48 percent of U.S. citizens opposed the war in Iraq. Should the president apologize? The president admitted that mistakes had been made in his address. He stated, "Our past efforts to secure Baghdad failed for two principal reasons: There were not enough Iraqi and American troops to secure neighborhoods that had been cleared of terrorists and insurgents." He also took responsibility for the mistakes by saying the situation, "that is unacceptable to the American people and unacceptable to me." Nevertheless, after all have been said and done, there was no apology made about the event of the Iraq war and its present outcome.

There is another side to this story. Most people have recognized that the President could not have initiated and sustained a war without some support. Most of us read about the Federal Government's checks and balances while in high school. We do not have to be political science experts to know that our U.S. Federal Government created three branches years ago as a means to establish limited powers for each branch. We learned that the Legislative branch, which includes the Senate and House of Representatives has the power to make laws, the Judicial branch, which encompasses the Supreme, Appeal and U.S. District Courts, interprets the laws, and the Executive branch, our President, is elected to office to administer them. The division of authority enables one branch to act as a check and balance on the other two. The idea of checks and balances within our Federal Government, like the division of State and Federal authority, has been modified by interpretation and usages, the basic structure or concept remain the same.

Although the war in Iraq against insurgencies, foreign fighters and others has not panned out as expected, both members of the Senate and House of Representatives have voted to support funding for our engagement in the affair. During the 2006 mid-term elections most congressional officials indicated that they opposed our continued commitment to the Iraq war. This was a mirror of the fact that public opinion polls conducted prior to the elections showed a vast majority of the people surveyed indeed opposed U.S. involvement in the war. Some of our political experts have interpreted the results of the 2006 mid-term elections as a signal from the American people to the President that they are totally dissatisfied with his policies in the Iraq war. The President's advisors have said that most citizens to do not understand the full ramifications of the war and what winning it really means to us and democracy in the area. Following the election, several congressional officials, especially those seeking higher offices, have offered half-hearted apologies for supporting the President's action in Iraq.

It probably was not the President's intention, but he and his administration inadvertently gave the American people a great lesson in political science. The President's decision to "stay the course" in spite of negative opinion polls, shift in party control in Congress following the mid-term election and recommendations presented by a special task force on the war is an indication that he does not value public opinion or voters presence.

Rehabilitation for Inappropriate Behavior

Most of our celebrities and other leaders recognize when they have created a disgraceful situation where they must offer an apology for their behavior. In addition to offering an apology some of them seek rehabilitation as a means to ameliorate their inappropriate behavior. After biting off part of boxer Evander Holyfield's ear in 1997, boxer Mike Tyson said he was seeking psychological help. The public never learned whether or not he actually received such help. We have not seen very much evidence that the psychological counseling indeed helped Mr. Tyson since he has been involved in several similar incidents thereafter. Actor Mel Gibson checked into a clinic for alcohol abuse after he was criticized for making an anti-Semitic remark upon being arrested. Actor/Comedian Michael Richards sought therapy for racist remarks made at a comedy club. Radio talk show host Rush Limbaugh sought help for painkillers addiction after it had been disclosed that he had obtained a large quantity of the pills illegally. Former U.S. Representative Mark Foley, who was forced to resign over his use of sexually explicit computer messages to congressional pages, announced through his attorneys that he had alcohol problems and was receiving treatment for the problem. His attorneys also took the opportunity to announce that Mr. Foley was gay and had been abused by a priest as a teenager. Former president of the National Association of Evangelicals, the Rev. Ted Haggard received rehabilitation treatment after allegations were made that he consorted with a gay prostitute and snorted meth. After apologizing for his involvement in the Jack Abramoff influence-peddling scandal, former Representative Bob Ney said he had checked into an alcohol-abuse program. News reports indicated that former President Bill Clinton sought help from the Rev. Jesse Jackson for his conduct in the Monica Lewinsky affair. Unknowingly at the time but the public learned sometime later was the fact that the Rev. Jackson had committed a similar cardinal sin. Representative Patrick Kennedy entered rehabilitation for addiction to prescription drugs in May 2006 after a nighttime car crash that he could not remember occurred. Actor Isaiah Washington who plays as a doctor on ABC's Grey's Anatomy show went into therapy for his use of an anti-gay slur against co-star T.R. Knight on the program's set.

It is not a big secret now-a-days that entertainers, politicians, media figures, religious and business leaders use apologies and rehabilitation services as a way to get on with their careers. They perform both acts before the public because they sense that these are what the public wants as a part of the so-called deal to continue in the professional areas they are engaged in. After the rehabilitation and/or therapy sessions have been documented, the over-riding issue becomes the apology or rehabilitation and not the underlining problems themselves, which caused the need for an apology in the first place.

Social experts say that psychological treatments for behavior problems can reap meaningful results for the individuals. For one helpful thing, they say is that the treatment provides an opportunity for the offending person to disappear from the public view for a period of time for wounds to heal. Therapy sessions can also help people who have a problem of saying and doing things they regret when they are angry. Sensitivity programs are designed to teach participants about how to be more receptive to diversity and learn more about what is acceptable in our society today.

Apology Blunders

As previously mentioned, sometimes a responsible person makes an attempt to apologize but end up not accomplishing the gesture. In some cases the apology tends to make things worse. Gilbert Keith Chesterton, British Journalist, Novelist and Poet, stated that, "A stiff apology is a second insult. The injured party does not want to be compensated because he has been wronged; he wants to be healed because he has been hurt." Words and statements are made but the end result leaves the offended and others confused. Boxer Mike Tyson's proposed apology to Evander Holyfield after biting off part of Holyfield's ear comes to mind as a good example. Tyson's statements, "Evander, I am sorry. You are a champion and I respect that," were appropriate under the circumstances. However, his statement of, "I am only saddened that this fight did not go further so that the boxing fans of the world might see for themselves who would come out on top," was most inappropriate because it did not indicate that he was saddened for committing the vicious unsportsmanlike act. The statements made by Mr. Tyson fell short of what is considered a genuine apology. Mr. Tyson did not apologize for hurting Mr. Holyfield. He merely said I am sorry, but sorry for what? He did not acknowledge that he caused harm to Mr. Holyfield nor promised that he would not let it happen again if the opportunity presented itself. It was noticed that Mr. Tyson did not show any sign of remorse toward Mr. Holyfield or other people following the incidents in which he caused harm.

During the early stage of collection of material for this book, I read in a local newspaper where a columnist wrote, "When religion gets into politics, the nation is in trouble." Some people strongly disagree with this statement. On the other hand, some of us have not given it much thought. However, our outlook on this issue is challenged when we read or hear statements that are made by religious leaders. Most people watch the news on television know the outspoken Rev. Pat Robertson, host of Christian Broadcasting Network's The 700 Club and founder of the Christian Coalition of America. He also has a large number of religious followers. When the Rev. Pat Robertson speaks on any subject, most viewers will associate his comments to religion. On an August 22, 2005 broadcast of The 700

Club, Rev. Robertson stated that if Venezuela's President Hugo Chavez thinks we (U.S.) are trying to assassinate him, we really ought to go ahead and do it.

After the broadcast, there was a great outcry from individuals and organizations' leaders for Rev. Robertson to apologize for his statements relating to assassination. Others felt he had spoken out of his area of expertise and had no justifiable cause to suggest such violence political actions. Still others campaigned to urge the ABC Family to stop showing the Rev. Robertson's 700 Club programs.

Two days later on August 24, Rev. Robertson published a press release on his web page as a means to clarify his statements and supposedly apologized for calling for the assassination of Chavez. His press release stated the following, "I want to take this opportunity to clarify remarks made on the Monday, August 22nd edition of The 700 Club where I adlibbed a comment following a very brilliant analysis by Dale Hurd of the danger that the United States faces from the out-of-control dictator of Venezuela, Hugo Chavez. In this story, Col. Chavez repeatedly claimed that Americans were "trying to assassinate him." In my frustration that the U.S. and the world community are ignoring this threat, I said the following: Thanks, Dale. If you look back just a few years, there was a popular coup that overthrew him; and what did the United States State Department do about it? Virtually nothing; and as a result, within about 48 hours, that coup was broken, Chavez was back in power. But we had a chance to move in. He has destroyed the Venezuelan economy, and he's going to make that a launching pad for communist infiltration and Muslim extremism all over the continent. I don't know about this doctrine of assassination, but if he thinks we're trying to assassinate him, I think we really ought to go ahead and do it. It's a whole lot cheaper than starting a war, and I don't think any oil shipments will stop. But this man is a terrific danger, and this is in our sphere of influence, so we can't let this happen. We have the Monroe Doctrine, and we have other doctrines that we have announced, and without question, this is a dangerous enemy to our south, controlling a huge pool of oil that could hurt us very badly. We have the ability to take him out, and I think the time has come that we exercise that ability. We don't need another 200-billion-dollar war to get rid of one strong-arm dictator. It's a whole lot easier to have some of the covert operatives do the job and then get it over with. Is it right to call for assassination? No, and I apologize for that statement. I spoke in frustration that we should accommodate the man who thinks the U.S. is out to kill him. Col. Chavez has found common cause with terrorists such as the noted assassin Carlos the Jackal, has visited Iran reportedly to gain access to nuclear technology, and has referred to Saddam Hussein and Fidel Castro as his comrades. Col. Chavez also intends to fund the violent overthrow of democratically elected governments throughout South America, beginning with neighboring Colombia. As I report the news daily from around the world, I am acutely conscious of the fact that our nation is at war. Not only are there active wars in Afghanistan and Iraq, but also there is a war of terror being waged against civilized nations throughout the world. We are in the midst of a war that is draining vast amounts of treasure and is costing the blood of our armed forces. I am a person who believes in peace, but not peace at any price. However, I said before the war in Iraq began that the wisest course would be to wage war against Saddam Hussein, not the whole nation of Iraq. When faced with the threat of a comparable dictator in our own hemisphere, would it not be wiser to wage war against one person rather than finding ourselves down the road locked in a bitter struggle with a whole nation? The brilliant Protestant theologian, Dietrich Bonhoeffer, who lived under the hellish conditions of Nazi Germany, is reported to have said: "If I see a madman driving a car into a group of innocent bystanders, then I can't, as a Christian, simply wait for the catastrophe and then comfort the wounded and bury the dead. I must try to wrestle the steering wheel out of the hands of the driver." On the strength of this reasoning, Bonhoeffer decided to lend his support to those in Germany who had joined together in an attempt to assassinate Adolf Hitler. Bonhoeffer was imprisoned and killed by the Nazis, but his example deserves our respect and consideration today. There are many who disagree with my comments, and I respect their opinions. There are others who think that stopping a dictator is the appropriate course of action. In any event, the incredible publicity surrounding my remarks has focused our government's attention on a growing problem which has been largely ignored."

The Rev. Pat Robertson went to a great extent to express why he made the statements pertaining to the assassination of Chavez. However, many people did not consider his statements a genuine apology. On August 25, Richard Cizik, vice president for governmental affairs at the National Association of Evangelicals, said that Rev. Robertson should apologize on his television show, The 700 Club, for his comments calling for the assassination of Venezuelan President Hugo Chavez instead of on his web page.

Another example where an attempt to apologize was performed poorly is the case involving Poland's Archbishop Stanislaw Wielgus. Prior to the Archbishop's installation ceremony in January 2007, he expressed regret for an act that he acknowledged "harmed the church." He further said, "I never informed on anyone and never tried to hurt anyone." His admission to cooperating with the secret police of the Communist era led to calls for the church to not install him as an Archbishop. The Archbishop's statement did not meet any of the elements that constitute a genuine apology. It was reported that he also made a statement that he was leaving his fate in the hands of Pope Benedict XVI. It probably would have been best if Archbishop Wielgus had not said anything at all about his role in dealing with the secret police of the Communist Party.

Still another example of an apology blunder is the case where the University of Nebraska football coach's proposed apology to the team fans for his coaching performance in its lost to the University of Oklahoma in the Big 12 championship game. The coach did not provide much specific in his statement. But a question remains after his statement, if his coaching performance had been what he wanted it to be, would it had made a difference in the outcome of the game?

An Apology Will be Forthcoming

It is almost certain that an apology will be offered by the offending person or organization following the disclosure of a major disgrace or horror act. Apparently, the U. S. Department of Army was under a considerable amount of pressure in December 2006 and early January 2007 to retain officers who had recently left the service. It was reported that mass mailing of letters to more than 5,100 officers mistakenly contained 275 (75 killed & 200 wounded) officers who had been killed or wounded in action in Iraq. The letters were sent to encourage the officers to consider returning to active duty. Senior Army officials were very disturbed by their blunder due to the use of the wrong database and offered a genuine apology to the affected individuals and family members. Gen. Richard Cody, Army Vice Chief of Staff, said that the mistake in mailing out the recruiting letters to soldiers who had been wounded and/or killed in actions was inexcusable and the Army would do better. He expressed empathy for the family members who received the letters. He also stated that the Army had immediately begun contacting each family to offer a personal apology for the error.

Sometimes our government and other high-level officials apologize for the wrong action. As example, in April 2007, Attorney General Alberto Gonzales offered a public apology to eight former federal prosecutors who had been fired by the Justice Department in November 2006. On one occasion, a report from the Justice Department indicated that the attorneys were removed because of poor performance. But a review of their most recent performance evaluations showed that most of them were recognized for outstanding accomplishments by the Justice Department. On another occasion, it was not made clear as to what basis was used to dismiss the attorneys from their positions. Attorney General Gonzales gave conflicting accounts about the dismissals of the eight U.S. attorneys. Initially, Mr. Gonzales said he was not involved in seeing any documents associated with the prosecutors' removal nor did he participated in any discussions about what was going on with them. At a news conference on March 13, 2007, he said basically he knew nothing about how the issue evolved. However, two weeks later, Kyle Sampson, former chief of staff to Mr. Gonzales, told a Senate Judiciary Committee that he and Mr. Gonzales discussed the status of removing the attorneys at least five times.

On April 15, 2007, two days before he was scheduled to appear before the Senate Judiciary Committee to answer questions regarding his conflicting statements, the Justice Department released a statement as a means to ameliorate the situation. Mr. Gonzales' statements were, "I have nothing to hide. I know that I did not, and would not, ask for a resignation of any individual in order to interfere with or influence a particular prosecution for partisan political gain. My statement about 'discussions' was imprecise and overbroad, but it certainly was not in any way an attempt to mislead the American people. The Justice Department owes them more respect than they were shown. This process could have been handled much better and for that I want to apologize."

Mr. Gonzales' last statement seems to imply that he only regrets how the process was handled. He failed to, 1) acknowledge what was done wrong by the Justice Department but mostly himself; 2) express ownership or responsibility for the controversy; 3) acknowledge impact of the actions caused the attorneys; 4) apologize for causing hurt and embarrassments to the attorneys; and, 5) promise that he would ensure that the action would not happen again while he is the Attorney General.

At the Senate hearing, Mr. Gonzales testified on many instances that he could not recall events he was asked to describe. Several people who attended the hearing stated that Mr. Gonzales used the "I do not recall" statement more than 75 times. On the other hand, he repeatedly defended the decisions themselves to fire the eight U.S. attorneys. We should never again question where people who are not attorneys learned how to be evasive.

A number of people accused District attorney Mike Nifong of Durham County, North Carolina, of over-reacting in charging three Duke University lacrosse players with rape of a stripper on March 13, 2006. The critics said his desire to be elected for the first time to the office he originally was appointed to was the primary motive for his actions. The players, their family members and attorneys labeled his actions as "offensive."

Several people described Mike Nifong as a tough-but-fair prosecutor. People who worked for and against him said he was a "hard-nosed prosecutor," who came to the courtroom prepared, organized and fair-minded. However, since the initial allegation of the rape by a stripper and indictments charges against the Duke's lacrosse players, a number of people said that he was taking a more proactive approach in the case due to political reasons.

The three accused players said they were innocent of any wrongdoings when the allegations were first made. All three said they had cooperated with police in their investigation of the allegations and were stunned that they had been indicted for a crime that never occurred. The three lacrosse players were charged with forcible rape and kidnapping as the accuser said the incident occurred at an off-campus house rented by the team for a party. The accuser identified the players as her attackers from photographs. The players' attorneys vowed that the charges would be proven wrong. They also stated that their clients would use DNA and other evidences to prove their case.

The allegations of rape by the young black female against the three white males raised attention and concerns within the Durham, North Carolina community along racial lines. The Durham, N.C. Trinity neighborhood where the alleged rape occurred already had a tense relationship with the university. School officials thought that by purchasing several buildings in the area would alleviate the problem. A committee created to review the lacrosse team behavior after the rape allegations recommended that the school should enforce stricter oversight and monitoring of players' conduct to correct behavioral issues often brought on by use of alcohol. The committee's report also said that there was a need for improvement in communication between the school's division of student affairs and the athletics department.

Thirteen months after the attack allegedly occurred, the charges against the three players were dropped. The accuser changed her story on how and what happened on March 13, 2006 several times. DNA tests and other evidences the prosecutor had could not link the players to a crime. North Carolina state Attorney General who was asked to take over the case mid-way through the investigation concluded that not only that Mr. Nifong's evidence was insufficient, but also that no attack took place. The state attorney general also labeled Mr. Nifong's actions in the case as "offensive."

In April 2007, Mr. Nifong issued a statement of support for dismissal of the charges and halfway apologized for his actions. He said, "To the extent that I made judgments that ultimately proved to be incorrect, I apologize to the three students who were wrongly accused." The players who were very angry, their families and attorneys did not accept Mr. Nifong's statements as a genuine apology.

Media reports in January 2007 revealed that former state House Speaker of Massachusetts, Thomas Finneran, admitted to obstruction of justice and apologized before a U.S. District Judge for playing an active role in developing plans for redistricting an area to dilute the impact of minority voters. Mr. Finneran offered an apology to all of the people of Massachusetts for his role in the plot. He said he embarrassed and shamed himself as well as his family. By committing the crime, he stated that it was a deviation from a life-long code of conduct he had made for his personal and professional life. Several family members and friends who were present at the hearing shed tears with him when he confessed to the act. Undoubtedly, the crying scenes compelled the Judge to be more lenient and spared the former state congressman prison time.

Even when the disclosure of a disgraceful situation is not considered major, there will be an apology forthcoming. This was evidenced in the case involving World Bank President Paul Wolfowitz who secured pay raises for his girlfriend at the State Department. Mr. Wolfowitz was criticized for helping negotiate large pay increases for a bank employee whom it was said he was romantically involved with. The friend of Mr. Wolfowitz was already at the bank when he came as president in 2005, leaving his position as deputy Defense Secretary. The bank regulations prohibit employees from supervising another person with whom they have a personal relationship. Consequently, the girlfriend had to be reassigned to another position outside the bank. The report stated that in the process of making arrangements for the reassignment to the State Department, Wolfowitz actively participated in the negotiation to get her a pay increase for more than $60,000. He apologized for his role in the negotiations process by saying, "In hindsight, I wish I had trusted my original instincts and kept myself out of the negotiations. I made a mistake, for which I am sorry." He made no mention of the fact that others may have been harmed by his actions, nor did he indicate that he would not commit the same offense again. Chairperson and other members of the World Bank Group Staff Association felt Mr. Wolfowitz had compromised the integrity and effectiveness of the World Bank and suggested that he resign from the position. On May 17, 2007, it was announced that Mr. Wolfowitz would resign his position as president of the World Bank at the end of June.

Apology Used as A "Safety Net"

Strange things do occur in real life. Sometimes we wonder who are stranger, people who supposed to be celebrities or us. Then we think about it for a minute and determine it is they. But tomorrow it may be us. Consequently, we must keep everything in proper perspective by doing the right thing right!

Near the beginning of this book, apology was defined as an acknowledgment of some fault, injury, insult, etc., with an expression of regret and plea for pardon. With the use of apologies and other statements to make everything right in our society today, an apology seems to have taken on a new meaning. A new peculiarity has emerged among people in the use of apology and other statements to escape further confrontations. It is noticeable that some people are using the apology gesture for other purposes than what the above definition indicates. The phrase, "safety net" may need to be added to the definition where it may be used as a form of protection against failure in the things we say.

Three examples can be cited where the "safety net" was needed and used for protection against further involvements. Curt Schilling who is a star pitcher for the Boston Red Sox baseball team, found use for the safety net approach when he issued a public apology to Barry Bonds, who is an outfielder for the San Francisco Giants for critical statements he made about Bonds on a radio interview in May 2007. The need for an apology or safety net was created when Schilling was asked if fans should hold their nose as Bonds closes in on the all-time home run record. Schilling said, "Oh yeah. I would think so. I mean, he admitted that he used steroids. I mean, there's no gray area. He admitted to cheating on his wife, cheating on his taxes and cheating on the game, so I think the reaction around the league, the game, being what it is, in the case of what people think. Hank Aaron not being there. The Commissioner, Bud Selig, trying to figure out where to be. It's sad." Following the radio interview, a number of people called and sent e-mail messages to Schilling to inform him a number of his statements about what Bonds had admitted to were not true. The Boston Red Sox manager, Terry Francona felt uncomfortable with the comments made by Schilling and met with him shortly afterward to address the issue. The next day, Schilling issued a statement that said, "Everyone has days and events in life they'd love to push the rewind button on, yesterday (Tuesday) was one of those days. Regardless of my opinions, thoughts and beliefs on anything Barry Bonds, it was absolutely irresponsible and wrong to say what I did. I don't think it's within anyone's right to say the things I said and affect other people's lives in that way."

The second example relates to a statement made by former President Jimmy Carter. On May 19, 2007, Mr. Carter was asked in an interview with the Arkansas Democrat-Gazette to rate the administrations of Richard M. Nixon and George W. Bush. Mr. Carter said, "I think as far as the adverse impact on the nation around world, this administration (George W. Bush) has been the worst in history. The overt reversal of America's basic values as expressed by previous administrations, including those of George H. W. Bush and Ronald Reagan and Richard Nixon and others, has been the most disturbing to me." Mr. Carter had second thoughts or considered the "safety net" technique immediately after his comments were published. The former President said his remarks about President Bush's foreign policy were "careless or misinterpreted." Mr. Carter said, "I wasn't comparing the overall administration, and I was certainly not talking personally about any president." Although Mr. Carter labeled his comments as being "careless," a White House spokesman rebuked the former President as "increasingly irrelevant," and stated that the comments were "reckless personal criticism" and unfortunate.

The third example also occurred in May 2007. Clinton Portis, who plays professional football for the Washington Redskins, made an attempt to defend Michael Vick, quarterback for the Atlanta Falcons, who was under investigations for allegations of holding dogfights at a home he owns. In the interview with the Virginia television station, Portis said, "I don't know if he was fighting dogs or not. But it's his property; it's his dogs. If that's what he wants to do, do it." Before the end of the same day, Portis issued the following statement, "In the recent interview I gave concerning dog fighting, I want to make it clear I do not take part in dog fighting or condone dog fighting in any manner."

Curt Schilling referred to a need to "push the rewind button," former President Jimmy Carter used the phrase, "careless or misinterpreted," and Clinton Portis used the statement, "I want to make it clear" of which all of them were using an apology or follow-ups comments as a safety net to avoid further connection with the subject issue.

Giving a Genuine Apology

Offering an apology is considered a social skill that we are taught and learned at home, school and put to practice at social events and in the public at large. Apologizing is an act we participate in and/or observe on almost a daily basis. The disturbing truth about apology is that most people do not know how to offer a meaningful apology. Most appalling is the fact that a great number of educated people have failed in making appropriate apologies. And not surprisingly, the educated people are the ones who are pitted in positions or situations in most cases where there are needs for apologies.

The appropriate manner in dealing with the gesture of offering an apology is very much similar to how we should approach any other type of problem, change or opportunity for improvement in the social world. Before we can effectively go about solving a perceived problem, we must first recognize that there is a problem or opportunity for improvement. Recognition is realized when we acknowledge that something is not right and something need to be done to rectify it.

The most important aspect of offering a genuine apology to someone or group that we have caused harm to is to first acknowledge within ourselves that we have caused harm to that person or group. The rest of the required actions to complete the process will come much less challenging. Most people know when they have hurt, caused inconvenience or insulted another. By acknowledging the harm to yourself, you will be able to show empathy toward the person you hurt and express regrets for doing so.

A genuine apology goes much farther than an admission that we did something wrong to another person or organization. Although important, an admission is just one step in the process required to offering a genuine apology. An example where an apology was not completely accomplished in this respect is the case involving nineteen freshman cadets at the Air Force Academy. The cadets admitted to cheating on a test of general knowledge about their branch of the military during the fall term in 2006. The tests will not affect the cadets' grade-point averages, but they must pass them to advance to the second year. Other cadets who did not cheat on the test reported the cheating in February 2007. Although the nineteen cadets' admission of obtaining answers to the test and forwarding them through an Internet social group and private computer messages after they were exposed, the gesture did not go far enough. Even though it was reported that the cadets would face an advisory panel that would suggest punishment measures, there was no mentioning that any of them offered an assurance to the Air Force Academy that the embarrassing action will not happen again.

Examples of a Genuine Apology

We do not have to become social scientists in order to be able to give a genuine apology. An example of a genuine apology can be demonstrated by revisiting the case involving New York Senator Alfonse M. D' Amato where the Senator apologized for remarks he made about Judge Lance Ito on a radio talk show on April 4, 1995. The Senator's first apology was not acceptable to most people. The second apology was much more appropriate and above board. He stated, "I'm here on the Senate floor to give a statement as it relates to that episode. It was a sorry episode. As an Italian-American, I have a special responsibility to be sensitive to ethnic stereotypes. I fully recognize the insensitivity of my remarks about Judge Ito. My remarks were totally wrong and inappropriate. I know better. What I did was a poor attempt at humor. I am deeply sorry for the pain that I have caused Judge Ito and others. I offer my sincere apologies." All of the required elements to justify a genuine apology were included in the Senator's second gesture. Upon having the opportunity to offer an apology, we can follow the same protocol shown above after acknowledging within ourselves that harm has been caused.

In order to illustrate how other genuine apologies can be presented to an offended person or group, we will revisit and use several of the cases that have been previously mentioned. First, it is important to recognize that the offender has acknowledged that there is a problem and secondly, that something needs to be done to ameliorate the situation. Also, the five elements previously given: 1) acknowledgment of what was done wrong, 2) express ownership or responsibility for the harm, 3) acknowledge impact the harm caused, 4) apologize for causing hurt, insult, or other harm, and 5) promise that it will not happen again; will be used to reconstruct the statements into genuine apologies.

Case: Michael Richards' use of the "N" word.

1) Acknowledge what was done wrong.

"I used racial remarks toward two individuals in response to what I considered was an attack on me as not being a good comedian."

2) Express ownership or responsibility for the harm.

"I was wrong in making those statements. After performing as an actor and comedian for many years, I should have known better and not made those kinds of remark."

3) Acknowledge impact the harm caused.

"My statements hurt a number of people's feelings, especially those of African American descent. I also caused an embarrassment to the comedy club."

4) Apologize for causing the hurt and embarrassment.

"I apologize for causing hurt and embarrassment in making those statements. I'm deeply sorry for acting the way I did."

5) Promise the action will not happen again.

"Please accept my sincere promise that this type of action will not occur again on my part."

Case: Mel Gibson's anti-Semite statements after being stopped by police for reckless driving.

1) Acknowledge what was done wrong.

"I used anti-Semite remarks when I was stopped by police officers last night."

2) Express ownership or responsibility for harm.

"I know what I said was greatly wrong. I failed a number of people when I made those statements ... including myself as I certainly know better."

3) Acknowledge impact the harm caused.

"My anti-Semite statements created a great amount of hurt for a large number of people who do not deserve this type of treatment."

4) Apologize for causing the insult and hurt.

"I am deeply sorry for the insult and hurt I caused all Jewish people throughout the world."

5) Promise the action will not happen again.

"I will never make those types or similar types of statements about any race again."

Case: Peter Cook, after it was learned he cheated on his wife.

1) Acknowledge what was done wrong.

"I admit that I cheated on my wife, Christie and there is no excuse for doing this wrong."

2) Express ownership or responsibility for harm.

"It was totally my fault for having an affair with another woman. I should have known better."

3) Acknowledge impact the harm caused.

"I am certain that this aberration caused a great amount of pain for Christie as well as to other family members."

4) Apologize for causing the hurt.

"I am deeply sorry for the pain and severe uncomforting feelings I caused my wife Christie and others."

5) Promise the action will not happen again.

"I have turned my life around and made a commitment that this type of action will not happen again."

Case: TV Evangelist Jimmy Swaggart, after he was caught on camera with a prostitute outside a motel.

1) Acknowledge what was done wrong.

"I was inappropriately involved with a prostitute at a motel. This action was wrong in consideration of all possible reasons."

2) Express ownership or responsibility for harm.

"I know that people, especially my wife and other family members and members of my congregation are disappointed in my disgraceful actions. It is my fault that I let them down."

3) Acknowledge impact the harm caused.

"My unfaithful actions created a great embarrassment for all people, especially for my family and Christians."

4) Apologize for causing hurt and embarrassment.

"I apologize for this horrible mistake and ask that all of you to forgive me for the hurt that I have caused."

5) Promise the action will not happen again.

"I have asked God to forgive me for this sin and I ask Him again in your presence. Lord, please forgive me for what I knew was wrong. I promise that I will not fail you in this way again."

Case: Boxer Mike Tyson, after biting off part of Evander Holyfield's ear.

1) Acknowledge what was done wrong.

"I bit off part of Evander Holyfield's ear in our fight last night."

2) Express ownership or responsibility for harm.

"I was wrong for biting Mr. Holyfield and there is no genuine excuse for doing it."

3) Acknowledge impact the harm caused.

"My actions in the boxing ring last night hurt not only Mr. Holyfield but the entire boxing sport as a whole. I also caused embarrassment to my family and manager in this incident."

4) Apologize for causing the hurt and embarrassment.

"I apologize to Mr. Holyfield for the pain I caused. Mr. Holyfield is the heavyweight boxing champion and I respect that."

5) Promise the action will not happen again.

"It is my intentions to seek professional help to preclude actions of this nature from happening again."

Case: Rev. Pat Robertson, statements made regarding suggestion to assassinate dictator Hugo Chavez of Venezuela.

1) Acknowledge what was done wrong.

"On our broadcast August 22, I suggested that we (U.S. military) ought to go ahead and assassinate President Hugo Chavez of Venezuela."

2) Express ownership or responsibility for harm.

"I was wrong for making the statements about assassination of President Hugo Chavez or the initiation of such actions toward anyone."

3) Acknowledge impact the harm caused.

"My statements hurt a number of people, especially Christians and those who advocate non-violence. I also caused a great embarrassment to religious leaders who oppose and teach against such actions."

4) Apologize for causing hurt and embarrassment.

"I apologize for making the inappropriate statements and for hurting and embarrassing the people whom I let down."

5) Promise the action will not happen again.

"Taking appropriate course of actions in addressing what should be done in dealing with a dictator of another country is the responsibility of the President of the United States and I respect that. In the future, I will limit my comments to only reporting what is happening in the world."

Interviews

Fred D. Gray, Attorney at Law:

Fred D. Gray truly does not need an introduction, but I will provide one anyway. More than the attorney who defended civil rights icons Rosa Parks and the Rev. Martin Luther King, Jr. More than the attorney who defended participants of the Montgomery Bus Boycott and the victims of the Tuskegee Syphilis Study. Far more than the attorney who has won scores of other civil rights cases in education, voting rights, transportation, health, and other areas, Fred David Gray has a special calling! He is a renowned attorney and an ordained minister.

Attorney Fred Gray was born and grew up in Montgomery, Alabama and had to leave the state to finish his education after earning his B.A. degree from Alabama State University in 1951 because blacks could not attend Alabama law schools at that time. He earned his LL.B. from Case Western Reserve University in 1954. After passing the bar examinations in Ohio and Alabama, Mr. Gray moved back to Montgomery to start his law practice where he announced that he was, "determined to destroy everything segregated that I could find."

Mr. Gray was one of a few lawyers in Alabama who took on civil rights cases during the late 1950s. He was one of the founders of the Montgomery Improvement Association (MIA) and handled all of the organization's legal affairs. He was also pastor of the Holt Street Church of Christ in Montgomery.

Throughout his legal career, Mr. Gray fought against segregation and discrimination. After the Montgomery bus boycott case, he took on other civil rights cases in Alabama where he represented local and state National Association for the Advancement of Colored People (NAACP), integration of higher education institutions, and Dr. Martin Luther King, Jr.'s tax trial.

Attorney Gray served in the Alabama state legislature from 1970 to 1974 as one of the first two African American elected since Reconstruction. In 1973, he introduced a bill to make the third Monday in January a state holiday in honor of Dr. Martin Luther King, Jr. The legislature did not approve the bill; however, the U.S. Congress declared Dr. King's birthday as a national holiday in 1984. Mr. Gray is the author of two books, "Bus Ride to Justice" and "Tuskegee Syphilis Study." As of this writing, he continues to practice law from his newly constructed office building in Tuskegee and from another office located in Montgomery, Alabama.

My interview with Attorney Fred Gray on March 6, 2007, was most rewarding and informative. Prior to the interview, it was my understanding that Mr. Gray had initiated an apology from President Clinton on behalf of the victims for the syphilis study. I started our discussion by asking two questions: Did you actually ask for an apology from the President on the Syphilis Experiment? Why ask for an apology especially when it had been documented that the government was wrong and the acts carried out were bordering on criminal offenses? My understanding of how the gesture was initiated was wrong. Mr. Gray retrieved a copy of his book, "The Tuskegee Syphilis Study" which was published in 1998 and referred to background information pertaining to the study. The book shows that on August 24, 1972, the federal government admitted wrongdoings and announced that the Tuskegee Syphilis Study Ad Hoc Panel would conduct an investigation.

The victims of the syphilis study asked Mr. Gray to represent them for securing an apology for the study after a group of them viewed an HBO's movie entitled, "Miss Evers' Boys." The dramatization of the study that focused in large measure on the role of the woman who worked with the participants was very upsetting to the participants as it made them angry, and gave them a feeling that they had been taken advantage of again. Mr. Gray represented the participants at a press conference on April 8, 1997 and denounced the movie.

> Mr. Gray's involvement in the apology is outlined in the book beginning on page 115. "I received a phone call from a news reporter in February 1997 asking me when President Clinton was going to make an apology to the participants in the Tuskegee Syphilis Experiment. The reporter assumed that since I represented the men, I would have some knowledge of the proposed apology. I did not. In fact, I was really shocked to hear that such a move was in the making without the involvement of the participants.
> More calls came from other reporters, convincing me that this was more than a rumor. When the original reporter made a follow-up call, I commented

that other reporters had been calling. Then it was her turn to be surprised. She said she had heard from a source, I later learned from an article in Jet Magazine that around this time the Congressional Black Caucus had asked the President to make an apology, which perhaps was behind the inquiries.

However, about the same time, Mr. Charlie Pollard's niece called and said someone from the Centers for Disease Control in Atlanta was coming over to see him. The CDC was the administrator of the Health Care and Death Benefit Program for the Study participants and certain of the heirs. I have an abiding interest in this program as I insisted that the health care program be made a part of the settlement agreement in Pollard v. United States to ensure that the benefits would continue regardless of changes in the White House or Congress. During the years immediately after the settlement, I knew the young ladies who worked on a day-to-day basis with the participants quite well. They kept me advised, and I kept them advised on the needs of the participants. However, as the CDC medical care became routine and as the number of surviving participants dwindled over the years, so did my contact with the Centers for Disease Control.

But, we learned that the CDC was also planning to visit other Study participants. Various members of my staff made arrangements to be present at these interviews, and afterward we concluded that the CDC was checking on the participants' health. This was done periodically. However, this could also determine whether the participants were in condition to travel to Washington, D.C. and learn the participants' current opinions of the health care program. During the interviews, no mention was made of an apology.

Within the next few weeks, two important events happened: First, I discovered that some eighteen months earlier, a Tuskegee Experiment Legacy Committee met on the campus of Tuskegee University, with one of its purposes to seek a Presidential apology. The committee was established without any input from or involvement by the Study participants. They were completely ignored. This was troublesome to them and to me because this typical of what whites have done to African Americans over the years. In too many cases, whites believed that they knew what was best for blacks, and blacks did not have to be consulted. Now, African Americans are following the patterns set by whites; now we don't consult each other.

Second, Miss Evers' Boys was shown on television, and several of the surviving participants held a conference at my law office to view a tape of the movie and to discuss a response. They asked me to write a letter to President Clinton advising him that the participants joined with others in requesting an apology. The letter should also ask that a permanent memorial be built in Tuskegee to recognize the role of the Study in the movement for human and civil rights. Finally, if the President elected to make such an apology, they wanted to be included in the planning and to an active part in any apology ceremony.

In addition, they asked me to arrange a press conference at one of the sites where they had been recruited for the study in 1932 so that they could tell the nation what they wanted as a result of their participation; they also wanted the country to know that they were joining with others in requesting an apology; and they also wanted to tell the nation that Miss Evers' Boys was inaccurate and did not properly portray them or Nurse Rivers.

In essence, the surviving participants, all men now in their nineties, decided they wanted to take control of any further public discussion of their lives. They asked me to help them, which I was only too happy to do. The first person I discussed this with, of course, was my wife, Bernice. Together, we began to make plans to implement their desires. We talked about it, prayed over it, and concluded that we would go ahead with the press conference the men had requested."

Mr. Gray felt that the apology by the President was important and necessary for the surviving participants and their families because most people in the country did not understand the nature of the study and what it had done to the victims. A great part of the misunderstanding regarding the Syphilis Study was a byproduct of the movie, "Miss Evers' Boys" which was grossly inaccurate.

Elbert P. Green, PhD, Retired Academic Administrator & Retired Major, U.S. Army:

Dr. Green was born in 1935 in Laneview, Virginia. He received a Bachelor of Science degree from Virginia State College in 1957, a Bachelor of Divinity degree from Felix Adler Memorial University in 1969, a Master of Science degree in Education from Troy State University, Montgomery, Alabama in 1988, a Master of Bible Philosophy degree from American Bible School at Kansas City, Kansas in 1968, and a PhD degree from Southwest University at New Orleans in 1991. Dr. Green entered the U.S. Army in 1958 as a Second Lieutenant and progressed through higher ranks to Major before retirement in 1979. He is also a certified teacher in the state of Alabama, certified hypnotherapies and an ordained minister. He was director of the Jr. ROTC at Indianola, Mississippi City Schools and held the same position at Macon County Alabama Schools. He also served as director of residence hall at Tuskegee University for six years.

Dr. Green is the author of four books: "Poetry of Gold" was published in 1982; "Poetry is Soul" was published in 1988; "Light of the World Is Poetry" was published in 1995; and "Daily Bread for Living" was published in 2004. He has contributed many articles for publication in newspapers and magazines over the past several years. He was inducted into the International Poetry Hall of Fame in 1997, Who Is Who of Contemporary Achievers Hall of Fame in 1997, Phi Beta

Sigma Fraternity Hall of Fame in 1999; and American Biographical Institute Hall of Fame in 2002. He currently holds membership in several professional and civic organizations in the Tuskegee, Alabama community. Dr. Green is married to Mary M and they have two children.

In serving as a career officer in the U.S. Army for more than 21 years, Dr. Green experienced and witnessed first-hand cases of insults and humiliations. During his tenure in the military, insults and humiliations were considered the rule rather than the exception. An apology in the military today is still most likely to be not acceptable, if one is offered, after a blatant act or an officer commits offense. As example, Army Capt. Derrick Roberson pleaded guilty in 1997 to having had consensual sex with a private. He apologized but was sentenced to 4 months in prison and dismissed from the Army, and his pension was revoked. He was the only officer among 10 soldiers at Aberdeen Proving Ground charged with criminal sexual misconduct.

Dr. Green was asked to express his views on asking for an apology, especially in cases where the President of the United States is asked to apologize for slavery. His first expression was that it was important to recognize the fact that we are empowering an individual when he or she is asked to make an apology for all and/or other people. He further stated that a person today, no matter what position he or she holds, couldn't genuinely apologize for something that happened centuries ago. However, he felt that past events, especially those horrible in nature should be recognized and shown for historical purposes. He mentioned that although enslavement of Blacks by whites has been documented for some time, very few people are aware of the fact that certain Native Americans owned slaves as well for many years.

R. Larry Fullwood, M.S.W., M.P.H., Retired Healthcare Director:

Mr. Larry Fullwood has had a unique and illustrated life and career work history. He was born in Flint, Michigan into a family of three boys and two girls. His father was a handsome Alabama playboy who left home looking for work during the depression and never returned. Larry was raised by his mother, Olivia, grandmother Pauline and step father Seth Lemuel, who died a young man of fifty-six, compliments of the General Motors foundry which was a mixed blessing of jobs and a beast that belched a pulse beat of smoke, soot and grime which penetrated and set the pace for the lives of everything that lived within a five hundred mile radius in every direction. Early on in life, Larry learned his survival skills on the playgrounds and the mean streets of a north-side St. John street ghetto in Flint where the most prevalent models of success were dope selling pimps and hustlers driving Cadillacs around the hood looking for recruits for their stables. Growing up in a gang infested environment where day to day experiences routinely included a host of life threatening near misses and close calls with both the street law and the law of the jungle, either of which could have resulted in death or hard prison time. It was a combination of mother and grandma's prayers and getting involved in Golden Gloves boxing. And also, his enlisting in the Air Force that provided an escape mechanism which enabled Mr. Fullwood to bypass a certain death sentence of being drafted into the Army and expiring in an infantry unit in Korea within a year of induction or dying from drugs and crime in the civil war streets at home.

As it has once been said, the rest of Larry's life is history … but not quite. After leaving the military, he attended college on the G.I. Bill with a hard nosed determination to stay out of the factory and off the streets which led to the following accomplishments: Two wives, two divorces, one son and four divine grandchildren.

Mr. Fullwood's education and training attainments include an Associate in Arts degrees from Mott Community College, Flint, Michigan and Los Angeles City College in Los Angeles, California; Bachelor of Arts from San Jose State College, San Jose, California; Master of Social Work from Washington University, St. Louis, Missouri, and a Master of Public Health degree from the University of Pittsburgh, Pennsylvania.

Thirty-one years of federal service including four years in the U.S. Force, SAC where he attained the rank of Staff Sergeant and was under the command of General Curtis LeMay, highlight Mr. Fullwood's work experience. The remainder of his federal service was in the capacity of Director, Associate Director and Clinical Social Worker for the Department of Veterans Affairs (VA) at five different VA facilities in the country. Mr. Fullwood retired from VA in September 1993 and since that time he has divided his time managing his investment portfolio, volunteering at church where he is a usher, working his flower gardens, chasing the sun in Florida and Arizona playing golf and reading at leisure.

Mr. Fullwood's life and work experiences have taught and positioned him to know a great deal about apologies and apologizing for something where harm has been done. Mr. Fullwood commented on President Clinton's apology for the Atlantic Slave Trade. "While I believe in apologies, I have set the value of an apology in my eye as only as valuable as the sincere gesture of forthright actions of payment of compensation for wrongs inflicted on an entire nation of black people on whose backs, blood, sweat and tears this nation was founded. Fortunes were build in this country by individuals and corporations whose benefactors remain among the wealthy and powerful elite who continue to set policy and guide the government and make command decisions that determine who lives and who dies and how they curse through the maze of worldwide tides, currents and winds that connect the land masses of planet earth. In my view, apologies are worthless without truth and accountability. Apologies are a negative number without corrective action to put the record straight and to do whatever is required to make the wrong right. Saying you are sorry for what you did and doing nothing about it is like putting salt on an open wound."

Guy M. Crawford, M.Ed., Retired School Principal:

Mr. Crawford was born and grew up in Monroe County Mississippi. His educational achievements include: Graduated from Monroe County Training High School, Amory, Mississippi; B.S. degree in Agricultural Education from Tuskegee University; and a Master degree in Education Administration & Supervision from Tuskegee University. Mr. Crawford also attained post-graduate studies at the Universities of Alabama, Kentucky and Oregon.

Mr. Crawford's professional assignments include the followings: Principal, Lee Junior High School, Union Spring; 1950 to 1951; Teacher, Lanier High School, Lanett, 1952 to 1957 and Lewis Adams, 1958 to 1962; Principal, Prairie Farm Elementary School, Shorter, 1963 to 1965; Principal, Shorter Elementary School, Shorter, 1966 to 1967; Principal, Nichols Junior High School, Tuskegee, 1968 to 1973; Principal, D.C. Wolfe High School, Shorter, 1973 to 1988; all within the state of Alabama.

Religious and community civic organizations affiliations include serving as an active member of the Bowen United Methodist Church in Tuskegee, Alabama, where he is the treasurer, member of the church and men choir and president of the senior choir. Mr. Crawford also serves in various capacities on the Alabama/ West Florida Conference of the Methodist Church. Other community involvements include member and advisor of the Boy Scouts of America; Phi Beta Sigma

Fraternity, Inc. where he has served as president of the local chapter on six occasions and as treasurer for five terms.

Mr. Guy M. Crawford is married to Jessie Knox Crawford and they have one daughter and two grandchildren.

As illustrated in Mr. Crawford's curriculum vitae, in serving as a teacher and principal in the various school systems, he has had numerous opportunities to counsel students on the appropriateness of apologies. As example, he has served as the adjudicator on many issues of conflict involving students at the schools. After hearing the issues, he recalls making decisions whereby one of the parties was informed that he or she owed the other party an apology for his or her wrongful actions.

Mr. Crawford feels that a person should never have to approach another person and ask or demand that he or she apologizes for a harm that has been caused by the offender. He thinks a person knows very well when he or she has hurt another person's feelings, especially when they reach high school age in life. The offender, he feels, should take his or her own initiative to confront the offended person and apologize if there is a genuine regret present for doing something wrong.

Doretha Lawrence Pero, Mortgage Corporation Owner:

Mrs. Doretha Pero, who is better known by family members and friends as "Dee," was born in Tallulah, Louisiana but grew up in Monroe, Louisiana. Her family moved to the city when she was 4 years old. She excelled in anything and everything in which she was given an opportunity to participate in. She was and still is an exceptional leader today. As Mrs. Pero was growing up it was said that she never picked a fight because she stood for right, but she earned a reputation of never backing down from a fight. She was known to whip girls twice her size and a few of the boys. Mrs. Pero left Monroe to attend college in Baton Rouge at Southern University A&M. She arrived at Southern University on the day of the famous Hurricane Betsy. She made the Deans' Honor Roll list in her freshman year, was initiated into Zeta Phi Beta Sorority during her Sophomore year, and graduated from Southern University in just three and a half years with a Bachelor of Arts degree in Business Administration and a minor in Economics. She graduated among those with the highest honors in the Business Administration class.

Mrs. Pero returned to Monroe after graduation from Southern University to seek employment. She was one of the few blacks who was hired to work at State Farm Insurance Company's home office, then located in Monroe, Louisiana. She worked herself ahead of everybody else in just one year and was considered for the position as a claim adjuster. However, at the same time, she had decided to take the high road and move to San Diego, California. Her first job in San Diego was as a bank teller trainee. She was the only student out of 30 that scored a perfect score on the teller examination and that accomplishment landed her a full-time position as a bank teller. She was the best at her job but was known as saying, "I knew that counting other people's money was not my destiny in life!" After taking a 5 weeks maternity leave after her first son was born she did not return to her banking job. She went to work for a Black owned Real Estate Broker in processing home loans. Although not required, she took and passed the real estate examination and received her real estate license. The rest of the story about this stupendous woman is history! Throughout her professional career, Mrs. Pero has been recognized as a proactive individual on accomplishing work related assignments. She progressed rapidly from a bank teller, to a loan processor, to manager of a major mortgage company, and Vice President of the mortgage lending division of a local bank. On December 3, 1990, a life long dream was fulfilled. Mrs. Pero founded her own company and named it, Premier Mortgage Corporation. She and husband Ernest, an active Real Estate Broker soon became known as gurus in the Real Estate and Mortgage Banking industries.

Mrs. Pero stated that having reached her professional goals, "It was at this time in my life that I had a real encounter with God." She discovered that God had his hand on her all the days of her life. She quotes *James 2:20,* "Faith without works is dead." She said unknowingly, she had both. She grew up in the church therefore, her faith came naturally, but she never shunned hard work. As a result, God honored His word. It was He who upheld her with His righteous right hand and caused her to excel effortless in all that she set out to accomplish. It was her personal encounter with God that led her to retire from her career in 1994. Her retirement gave her more quality time with her second son who weighed into this world at one pound fourteen ounces. She stated that she had a life changing experience. Mrs. Pero became a volunteer mom in the Special Needs Children classroom, became very active within the church, joined Rotary International, a service organization for the greater good of mankind, and became a trustee board member of San Diego Youth Involvement.

When she was asked to comment on her greatest accomplishments in life as a professional person, she stated, "In spite of all of my professional accomplishments, my passions in life are studying the Word of God, helping others to come into the full knowledge of Jesus Christ and traveling abroad and throughout the United States. She stated with conviction that she considered her greatest achievements in life were her visits to Jerusalem, the Holy City, Capital of Israel, having "walked where Jesus walked" and having been re-baptized at the Jordan River, in October 1998.

Mrs. Pero believes that one should never ask or demand an apology. A genuine apology comes from the heart and is spontaneous. When harm has been done to someone the person inflicting the harm should readily offer an apology. Mrs. Pero states that a demanded or coerced apology is like one that has not loved as described in I Corinthians 13:1. The apology becomes like sounding brass or a clanging cymbal. Although she did not apologized in her younger days, she wants to offer a sincere apology to all of the girls she beat up while in elementary school in Monroe, Louisiana. She stated that she regrets to be in the position of having to apologize to anyone; however, as a staunch Christian, she believes a sincere apology is a way to bring the light of Christ to a lost and dying world.

Harry T. Statham, MS, Retired Federal Investigator:

Mr. Harry T. Statham was born on June 21, 1918 in Hamlin, Texas. At birth, his father was serving in the United States Army in France during World War I. He was the oldest of nine children, including 8 boys and one girl.

Mr. Statham had lived in four states by the time he reached the age of 12. His family moved to Rayville, Louisiana shortly after his 12th birthday where he finished high school at Rayville High in 1938. He received a Master of Accounting degree in 1947 from Columbus University, located in Washington, D.C.

In November 1941, Mr. Statham began a career with the General Accounting Office (GAO) after receiving a job offer from the federal agency. Has starting salary was at the General Schedule (GS)-1 level $90.00 a month or $1,080.00 annually.

The Government Accountability Office (GAO) is the non-partisan audit, evaluation, and investigative arm of Congress, and an agency in the Legislative Branch of the United States Government. The GAO was established as the General Accounting Office on June 10, 1921 by the Budget and Accounting Act. GAO's current mission statements indicates that the agency exists to support the Congress in meeting its constitutional responsibilities and to help improve the performance and ensure the accountability of the federal government for the benefit of the American people.

GAO examines the use of public funds, evaluates federal programs and activities, and provides analyses, options, recommendations, and other assistance to help Congress make effective oversight, policy, and funding decisions. Over the years, GAO has been recognized as "The Watchdog of Congress" and "The Taxpayers' Best Friend" for its frequent investigative reports that have uncovered waste and inefficiency in government.

Most of Mr. Statham's work with GAO involved investigative field assignments. A majority of the studies and reviews he participated in were initiated by requests from members of Congress. His investigative assignments deployed him to such places as Guam and Puerto Rico and other unincorporated territories of the U.S. He transferred form GAO after 20 years of service to the Federal Maritime Commission (FMC) to continue to work as an investigator within that agency. FMC is an independent federal agency, based in Washington, D.C., responsible for the regulation of ocean borne transportation in the foreign commerce of the U.S. During his last ten years with FMC, Mr. Statham served as director of the agency's Gulf Region. He retired from the federal government on August 30, 1980 after 18 and half years with FMC and a combined total of 39 years of federal service.

Mr. Statham married his lovely wife, the former E. Elizabeth Cumpton on July 12, 1942. They have no children. They are members of the First United Methodist Church of Monroe, Louisiana. Mr. Statham has served on most of the boards of the church as well as the church's manager, in a volunteer status and is currently serving as investment manager of the permanent endowment fund for the church. He has attended the Louisiana's annual conference of the United Methodist Church each year for the past 30 years. He served on the finance committee for 8 of those years and 16 years on the board of pensions.

Mr. Statham joined the National Association of Retired Federal Employees (NARFE) shortly after retirement in 1980. He has served in various positions within the organization for more than 27 years. He has served as President of the

Monroe chapter of NARFE for more than 10 years and was president of the state federation for 2 years.

The above background information disclosures that Mr. Statham has had a wide range of experiences in dealing with people from a variety of cultures. In his work experiences, he has witnessed instances where apologies have been made for various reasons.

In my interview with Mr. Statham regarding apologies, I asked that he not be influenced by my personal view opinion on the subject. He stated, "I agree with you. One should never ask or demand an apology. If the offender were a friend, I would ignore the offense, hoping he or she would apologize after giving more thought to what he/she had done. If the person was not a friend, I would end my relations I had with him or her."

Never ask or Demand an Apology

A number of authors who have written on the subject of apology suggested that we should learn how to ask for an apology. They support this position by saying we should not distance ourselves from those who have offended us and failed or refused to apologize. It is further stated that by asking for an apology, we can close the gap that was created by the offense. It is my position that an apology should be spontaneous and not coerced or asked for. This position is based on the theory that a person with a sound mind will show compassion toward another and apologize when he or she learns that another person's feeling has been hurt by his or her action.

It is important to state that the law assumes a person to be of sound mind until evidence is given meeting the legal standard for incompetence and a finding of incompetence is made. However, the legal standard for incompetence has differences, primarily depending upon the particular purpose involved. It must be recognized that society generally does not assume a person to be sound mind based on legal evidence. Consequently, if a person act in a deviance manner, most likely society (people within the community) will label the person as insane whether or not a finding of incompetence has been made. In the observation of deviance behavior, society will go so far as to indicate that the person's "elevator does not go all the way to the top."

By appropriate means, the offended person should let the offender know that he or she has been hurt and end further action after that. After informing the offender that his or her statements have hurt you and/or actions, the ball is then in the offender's court. Sometimes, distancing ourselves from the offending person is the best decision to make. Undoubtedly, some people are just plain ignorant ... including some of our relatives, and we will never be able to make them understand the value of an apology. Even worse, we will not be able to convince certain people that there is a proper way (correct) and an improper (incorrect) way to relate to others. Most people in the civilized world have had lessons on apology and some have even taken courses on apology and etiquette at the high school and college levels. Most people will readily apologize when they have recognized or been informed that they have offended someone. Others will recognize their wrongdoing and make a stab at apologizing for offending another. Others will make an attempt to apologize in good faith but end up making the offense worse. Still others will refuse to apologize or even acknowledge the offense altogether. Some people never would want to hurt another person's feelings and just the thought that they may have hurt another person would greatly hurt them upon learning that another person had been offended by something he or she had said or done.

I strongly agree with the five reasons why apologizing to another person is important. The five reasons put apologizing in proper perspective that it: 1) shows respect, 2) shows that the person is capable of taking responsibility for his or her actions, 3) shows that the person cares about the other person's feelings, 4) shows that the person is considerate and empathizes with other people, and 5) apologizing disarms the other person and may eliminate anger. Both giving and receiving an apology are important. However, to ask or demand an apology is presumptive and is like saying to the offender, "you have a guilty conscience. You must regret that you caused me pain and/or sufferings. You broke up our relationship or association. If you don't want to be punished or looked down on by others, you must apologize to me."

When a person says to another, "You owe me an apology." Or make the statement, "I demand that you apologize for doing what you did." He or she is treating the issue as a debt. The dictionary defines debt as, "something owed by one person to another. An obligation to pay or return something." Owe means to be indebted to (someone) for a specified amount or thing. The need for an apology is not a debt because law cannot enforce the payback or regrets.

One of the primary reasons I recommend to never ask for an apology is the fact that in a vast majority of the cases where one is asked for the offending persons knew they had created a situation where harm had been made. The harm was advanced to hurt or humiliate one person or group in order to showcase or promote another person's mission. An example to support this contention is found in the actions of former Alabama Governor George C. Wallace.

Alabama's history indicates that George C. Wallace started his political career in the state as a liberal. In the early days of his career, he was considered one of the most liberal judges in Alabama, and a moderate on racial issues. But being moderate on racial issues in Alabama in the 1950s, 1960s, and 1970s would not get anyone very far in politics. It did not take long for Mr. Wallace to learn that being moderate was an obstacle. He also loved the limelight and was driven by a hunger for power. After losing his first attempt to be governor, Mr. Wallace initiated a mission where he was willing to do and say whatever it took to position himself to better his own state of affairs in politics. He saw racism as the salvation for a political career that had stalled up to that point. He knew that playing the race card in Alabama would excite many people … especially a majority of the white people. Playing the race card and saying what people wanted to hear propelled him to power.

"Segregation now, segregation tomorrow, and segregation forever" was the great rallying cry by Mr. Wallace. After he was elected governor of Alabama in 1962, Mr. Wallace was immediately thrust into center stage in the national drama of civil rights, playing to the crowds, playing to the cameras, "standing in the schoolhouse door," if in an attempt to stop two black students from enrolling.

History also indicates that a storm of racial violence erupted following Mr. Wallace's attempts to exploit blacks. The jeering mobs, the fire hoses and dogs as seen on television, the cold-blooded murder of Sunday school children, the police brutality of Bloody Sunday at Selma Alabama were seared forever on the nation's memory. His speeches resonated and echoed the emotions of his audience. He knew exactly what words to say and the right place to express them. A vast majority of the people in Alabama felt he was saying and doing the right thing.

Undoubtedly, Mr. Wallace knew his speeches and racial actions hurt a number of people during his political career. History does not indicate that he was asked to apologize for his offensive actions. However, it does show that he took the initiative to apologize later in his life for his earlier political depressive actions. In October 1996, the former Alabama governor met with Mrs. Vivian Malone Jones in Montgomery prior to honoring her with an award named in memory of his wife that recognizes women who made major improvements in the state. Mrs. Jones was the Black woman Mr. Wallace tried to keep out of the University of Alabama with his "standing in the schoolhouse door" protest in 1963. The former governor apologized to Mrs. Jones and said, "Vivian Malone Jones was at the center of the fight over state's rights and conducted herself with grace, strength and above all, courage. She deserves to be rewarded for her actions in that air of uncertainty." Mrs. Jones later said, "There is no question Wallace and I will be remembered for the stand in the schoolhouse door. There is no way you can overcome that. But the best that can happen at this point is to say it was a mistake. We all make mistakes. He said he felt that it was wrong, that it shouldn't have happened. He said he felt the state of Alabama is better now than it was then as a result of what has happened through the integration and the desegregation of the schools here."

A documentary of the George C. Wallace's political career was shown on Public Broadcasting Service (PBS) television in a series during the late 1990s. The documentary was followed by an Internet web-page opinion transcript whereby people could express their views on the former governor. Many viewers commended Mr. Wallace for his accomplishments as governor and for having the courage and convictions to apologize for prior depressive actions. Many others expressed regrets that he did not recognize the shortcomings and harm he caused many people at the time when the harm was afflicted upon the people.

As previously indicated, most people know when they have created a situation where they should offer an apology for their bad behavior. However, pride and other motives get in the way and they refuse to give one … especially at that particular time. Pride is defined as an unduly high opinion of oneself or exaggerated self-esteem. Without questions, pride is the hardest thing for some of us to swallow.

Former Governor George C. Wallace completed what is considered a successful political career by using the race card. Another politician, former U.S. Senator George Allen was not as successful and found that the use of words and symbols, including the Confederate flag, could be offensive to racial minorities. More damaging than expected, his expressions and use of symbols played a pivotal role in his re-election lost in November 2006.

According to news reports, Mr. Allen wore a Confederate flag pin on his lapel in his 1970 graduation picture from a Southern California high school. He hung a noose from a plant in his Charlottesville law office in the 1980s and a Confederate flag inside his home. As governor in the mid-1990s, he alienated some by signing a resolution that designated a Confederate history month in Virginia but did not acknowledge the evils of slavery. Mr. Allen said he did not see racial overtones in the Confederate flag. He said he was a rebellious youth and viewed the banner as a "symbol against authority." As a history major at the University of Virginia in the early 1970s, he said, he also began to see the flag as a proud heritage symbol for those with ancestors from the South who fought in the Civil War. "What I appreciate, and wish I had sooner, is that that symbol, which for me was fit for simply rebelling against authority, and for others was fit for pride in heritage, was and is for black Americans an emblem of hate and terror, and emblem of intolerance and discrimination," he said.

Questions about Mr. Allen's racial sensitivity was raised again when he called a campaign worker of his opponent a "macaca." Macaca is the name of an Eastern hemisphere monkey and is considered a slur in some cultures. Mr. Allen repeatedly apologized, saying he was unaware of the word's meaning. The incident drew national attention and indignation. Mr. Allen said, "I've learned a valuable lesson about the power of words, about how words carelessly chosen, or in my case, even made up, can have a totally unintended meaning and impact for another person from another background or from a different cultural perspective." He also said, "In a careless moment, I fell short of my own standards, of my own positive way of living and what I strive and aspire to be."

Mr. Allen apologized again for the remark before about 300 black educators attending a national conference for officials from historically black colleges and universities. He said, "The point is, symbols matter, they should matter, and this is something that I wish I learned a lot earlier. Even if your heart is pure, the things you say and do and the symbols you use do matter because of the way others may take them."

The preceding example of an apology pertaining to the challenge addressed by former Senator George Allen conveys the point vividly that we should not ask for an apology from a person that has offended us. As far as I could tell from research, no one asked Senator Allen to offer an apology for what he said or did. Why not? There was no genuine need to do so. Mr. Allen recognized within himself long before the first apology was offered on the subject that harm and hurt had been made. People were hurt and humiliated by what he had said and done over the years leading up to the public disclosure. Eventually, it all came to a head and had a sad ending. I truly believe that Mr. Allen regretted using the Confederate flag and making offensive statements that alienated some people.

There is one interesting fact that is unclear and hard to understand about the George Allen case. As well known, all politicians, especially those at the state and national levels, have advisors to assist them in dealing with various issues, problems and opportunities for improvement. It is very much hard to understand why one of Senator Allen's advisors did not call him aside and informed him that certain statements and actions he was employing were offensive to certain people. A genuine supportive and loyal advisor would have taken the initiative to inform the Senator ... whether he wanted to hear the advice or not.

A demand for an apology by a person or group is a strong statement and in many instances is not necessary. The right thing to do in a majority of the cases is simply let it be known that you or the group of individuals had been offended by the offender. An example to illustrate this is the case involving a statement made by Gen. Peter Pace, Chairman of the Joint Chiefs of Staff regarding homosexuality. In an interview with the Chicago Tribune newspaper in March 2007, Gen. Pace stated, "I believe that homosexual acts between individuals are immoral and that we should not condone immoral acts. I do not believe that the armed forces of the United States are well served by saying through our policies that it's OK to be immoral in any way." The next day after the interview, Gen. Pace expressed regret for calling homosexuality immoral. He did not apologize but did say that he should have focused more in the interview on the Pentagon's policy about gays and not on his personal views.

Secretary of Defense Robert Gates expressed displeasure with the General's statement for criticizing homosexuality by saying, "Personal opinions have no place in the military."

Certain gay advocacy groups, such as the Service-members Legal Defense Network demanded an apology from Gen. Pace, saying, "Gen. Pace's comments are outrageous, insensitive and disrespectful to the 65,000 lesbian and gay troops now serving in our armed forces." Demanding an apology was an act of going too far and overly provocative on the part of the gay groups. The groups' expression simply should have been that they were disappointed in the General's statements about homosexuality and disrespect the statements reflected upon lesbian and gay troops serving in the military. After making such an expression, the ball would then be in the General's court to apologize or not apologize for what he said. One should never come across as he/she is forcing an individual to apologize ... no matter how severe the offense may seem. By doing so the element of genuineness is contaminated for the reason that the offender probably had no plans to apologize.

Several years ago, I was asked to make an apology for a statement I made in a meeting but I refused to apologize. Shortly after I was appointed to serve as medical center director at the Tuskegee VA Medical Center in 1986, a doctor at the nearby VA medical center informed me that I owed him an apology for something that I said at a meeting. I refused to offer the doctor an apology because I did not feel one was warranted. The two VA medical centers (Montgomery & Tuskegee) are only 35 miles apart and both medical centers had inpatient and outpatient care surgery services at the time. Consequently, as an initiative to maximize utilization of resources and reduce and/or eliminate redundancy, the regional director mandated that the two medical centers develop plans whereby certain services could be eliminated at one and strengthen at the other. The plans also would require changes and improvements in referral policies.

The mandate necessitated a need for meetings between top management officials from the medical centers to focus on development of the plan. At the first meeting, the doctor, who was serving as Chief of Staff at the Montgomery medical center, stated to me in the opened discussion that the veterans (patients) had told him that they do not want to go to the Tuskegee medical center for treatment because the facility was not clean. I made no comments in response to the statement. At the second meeting assembled to discuss the same initiative, the doctor made a similar statement, indicating that patients had informed him that they did not want to be referred to the Tuskegee medical center for treatment because the facilities were not clean. I made no comments regarding the statement although I had learned it was not true after a personal walk-through and discussing the issue with responsible staff at the medical center. In our third meeting we had reached the stage where definitive recommendations would be finalized for considerations of the regional director. Again, the doctor stated that patients had informed him that they do not want to be referred or transferred to the Tuskegee medical center for treatment because it was not clean. On this occasion, I took the opportunity to respond to the doctor's statement. I stated to the doctor by first calling his name and repeated the statement he made. Then, I said he personally knew the statement was not true because he had worked at the same Tuskegee medical center for more than 25 years prior to assuming his current position as Chief of Staff at the Montgomery medical center. I reminded him that he spent 20 of the 25 years serving as Chief of Surgical Service. I mentioned that according to my discussions with the Chief of Environmental Management Service at the medical center, the doctor never expressed dissatisfaction with cleanness in his work area. I also informed the doctor that since he was very much familiar with the physical plant at the medical center, he should have refuted the patients' statement on cleanness and/or upkeep. Approximately three days following the meeting I received a letter from the doctor demanding that I apologize for making the statements I made at the last meeting. Of course I did not apologize but I did respond to his letter and informed him that everything I said at the meeting was true. I also informed him in my response that his ulterior motive for making the statements regarding patients' denial for treatment at the Tuskegee medical center was wrong.

By not asking for an apology from someone who has hurt you does not mean you are weak in character or not able to speak up for yourself. We can easily tell a person (if such an act is possible) that he or she has treated us with disrespect, inconsideration or some other wrongs without asking for an apology.

On January 31, 2007, the State of Virginia's Legislature took steps to move toward enacting a measure to apologize for slavery at the state level. Certain individuals and groups have been petitioning for several years to obtain a national formal apology on slavery from the President. In concert with my views that have already been expressed, I totally disagree with asking the President of the United States to make a formal apology for slavery. This opinion is not based so much on the fact that the President and none of the current members of both houses of Congress had nothing to do with slavery, we should acknowledge the fact that an apology will not cure or solve a single existing problem we now have, including emotions, regarding ownership or exploitation of another person. Consequently, our time, efforts and financial resources should be directed toward ameliorating current loitering racial unfairness.

The Virginia Legislature unanimously approved a measure that expressed "profound regret" for the state's role in the slave trade and other injustices against African-Americans and Native Americans. Del. Donald McEachin, whose great-grandfather was a slave, sponsored the measure. Mr. McEachin felt that the bill was important at the time because the state of Virginia was celebrating the 400th anniversary of the founding of Jamestown in 2007, America's first permanent English settlement. The site was also the first entry point for African slaves in America.

As expected, all Virginia legislators were not in agreement with an apology for slavery. Del. Frank Hargrove, Sr. stated that, "Blacks should get over slavery instead of seeking a formal apology from the state." Further, he stated that he voted for the revised measure because, "It expresses regret without apologizing for anything." Sometimes this is what we get … "nothing" when we ask or make strong demands for an apology. Mr. Bruce Gordon, while serving as president of the National Association for the Advancement of Colored People (NAACP), expressed a point of view similar to my own. He said, "An apology alone does not heal wounds. It's important to recognize past wrongs, it's more essential to fix lingering racial inequities."

The state of North Carolina followed Virginia's lead in apologizing for promoting slavery. The North Carolina Senate apologized on April 5, 2007 for the Legislature's role in promoting slavery and Jim Crow laws that denied basic human rights to the state's black citizens. The Senate unanimously backed a resolution acknowledging, "profound contrition for the official acts that sanctioned and perpetuated the denial of basic human rights and dignity to fellow humans." Majority Senate Leader, Tony Rand, sponsored the legislation for the apology. He felt that the apology would help make the lawmakers of the state better children of God and representatives of all people of the state of North Carolina. The North Carolina House of Representatives had to effect approval action in order for the measure to be formalized.

Out of all fairness in respect to those who believe the President of the United States should offer a formal apology for slavery, I include an article written by Dr. Carol M. Swain for the Washington Post on July 16, 2005. Dr. Swain is a professor of political science and law at Vanderbilt University and a visiting fellow at Princeton University. The title of his article was "An Apology for Slavery." He wrote the following: "It's time for the Republican Party to write a new chapter in race relations. What I have in mind is something beyond the Senate's recent resolution on lynching and this week's expression of regret by a high-ranking Republican official for the GOP's use of what came to be known as the "Southern Strategy." What I propose is a formal apology for slavery and its aftermath. This could take the form of a joint resolution passed by both houses of Congress and signed by the president in a ceremonial setting where Americans could gather to symbolically bury their past.

Whenever the idea of an apology is raised, some whites reflexively recoil. They believe it is a bad idea because it conjures up images of innocent whites prostrating themselves before blacks for crimes they never committed. Most outspoken are whites whose ancestors arrived after the end of slavery and those who fought for the Union. Neither we nor our ancestors, they argue, had anything to do with slavery, so why should we apologize?

Others will say that an apology is not necessary because one has already been issued—two, really. In 1998 President Clinton acknowledged the evils of slavery. And last year President Bush visited Goree Island, a holding place for captured slaves in Africa, and spoke of the wrongs and injustices of slavery. "Small men," he said, "took on the powers and airs of tyrants and masters. Years of unpunished brutality and bullying and rape produced a dullness and hardness of conscience. Christian men and women became blind to the clearest commands of their faith and added hypocrisy to injustice."

That sounds like an apology. Nevertheless, while presidents as far back as John Adams have acknowledged the wrongness of slavery, there is still much to be said for an official apology. It would bring closure and healing to a festering wound.

President Bush is the right man for the job. Since he cannot run for reelection, he can't be accused of pandering for votes. Because he is a born-again Christian, he can and should do this. Since most blacks are Christians, they would graciously accept the apology. By issuing an apology, President Bush could dramatically improve race relations and his party's standing among African Americans.

A national apology would be a collective response to a past collective injustice, and would imply no culpability on the part of individuals living today. America as a nation would apologize for allowing slavery within its borders, with no individual present-day party being singled out for blame.

Already, our failure to acknowledge such a blatant wrong has set us apart from other great nations that have expressed contrition for misdeeds. Consider Germany, which has apologized for the suffering caused by its actions toward Jews and others. More recently Tony Blair apologized on behalf of Britain for its treatment of the Irish during the potato famine of the 1840s. Pope John Paul II apologized for the past sins of the Roman Catholic against non-Catholics. Australia apologized for its mistreatment of the country's aborigine population. What, then, would be the great harm in our apologizing for slavery and the Jim Crow racism that followed? Opponents will sometimes argue that an apology would open the door to claims for monetary reparations. But a national apology would do no such thing. To begin with, the very legality of slavery before passage of the 13th Amendment would make a claim in tort proceedings highly dubious. Then there is the problem of the statute of limitations having long expired. An additional impediment would be the absence of a living wrongdoer to prosecute. Legal precedent is against it. There is little chance that an apology would trigger the legal liability its opponents claim.

There are no good reasons to oppose a national apology for slavery and plenty of good ones to support it. We would all reap enormous national and international rewards from such a goodwill gesture. The Republican Party would perhaps reap the most. An official apology would offer the party the opportunity to reclaim the mantle of the party of Lincoln by forging a new relationship with African Americans, and not clouded by the spectacle of Willie Horton or Trent Lott. And it would do immeasurable good in terms of improving race relations. Best of all, it wouldn't cost a cent. That's a pretty good deal all around."

In January 2007, state Representative Mary Margaret Oliver, introduced a resolution in the Georgia Legislature to apologize for the state's authorization of sterilization of 3,300 inmates, state mental patients, and others. The sterilizations took place between 1937 and 1970, when Georgia and many other states were seeking to improve the human race by eliminating supposed hereditary flaws such as mental illnesses and physical deformities. The Atlanta Journal Constitution newspaper (ajc.com) reported that, "State lawmakers have introduced a resolution calling on the House of Representatives to declare 'its profound regret for Georgia's participation in the eugenics movement and the injustices done under eugenics laws.'" State Representative Oliver stated, "The better job we do of recognizing our history, the better job we can possibly do in the future and understand where we need to go." I strongly agree with that statement. And rather than apologizing for slavery, sterilizations and other gross injustices, we (state Legislatures) should recognize these horrible incidents and assess where we need to go from that point and time. It is not as easy as Del. Frank Hargrove, Sr. may suggest in that, "Blacks citizens should get over slavery." Horrible incidents such as slavery, the Holocaust, sterilizations, and fake medical treatment (Syphilis Experiment) are just a few of the dreadful and shocking incidents buried in our world's history and should be brought out and recognized as such. The incidents happened and they will not go away if we do not talk about them.

Sometimes it is almost impossible to ask for an apology from a person who has offended you. While serving as an associate medical center director at two medical centers and later as medical center director in VA, several times I received offending inappropriate remarks from people I did not know nor did many of them knew who I was. Even after explaining to them who I was and what my job was, made little or no difference in how the offending persons felt about the remarks they made. I learned that some people seem to enjoy the fact that they could offend or humiliate another person just because they had the privilege and opportunity to do so. I also learned that certain people would never accept the fact that what they said or did pertaining to another person was offensive as far as they were concerned.

I Did Not and Will Not ask …
to Apologize for …

I will not ask my granddaughter, Courtney to apologize for not recognizing me after I had allowed my beard to grow long and it had turned gray-white. At six months old, she assumed I was her grandfather because we told her so. But at nine months she refused to let me hold her. She only would stare at me. I imagined that she must have thought that I was an outer-space monster! Bless her little heart.

I will not ask my neighbors in Lincoln Park to apologize for reneging on our culvert project. Most of them had agreed to participate in the community-wide initiative for installation of culverts where there were opened ditches as a means to improve the aesthetics environment, health and safety conditions. However, after working with the Ouachita Parish Police Jury to obtain a waver on payment on fees for the survey, only three citizens out of 125 households went down to sign up. Undoubtedly, their inactions indicated that they placed no value on improving living conditions in the community.

I will not ask my neighbor for an apology who allows his dog to run out late at night so it can deposit its waste on my lawn. The dog may not be aware of the nature of the situation but the owner does.

I will not ask another neighbor for an apology who walks his dog through the neighborhood and allows the dog to deposit its waste in other people's yards when no one is watching. The primary purpose for walking the dog through the neighborhood is for it to deposit the waste in another person's yard and not for the exercise.

I will not ask Monroe City Councilman Arthur Gilmore, Jr. for an apology for not responding to my inquiry regarding how he was going to implement installment of culverts in the opened ditches in his District. During the Councilman's reelection campaign in 2004 he stated that one of his future goals was to install culverts in the opened ditches throughout the area. The Councilman was sent a letter on April 20, 2004. He never responded to the letter nor was it returned as undelivered.

I will not ask the Monroe Postmaster to apologize for not being responsive to our request of January 2006 for a post office or substation in southeast Ouachita Parish. Three letters were sent to the Postmaster describing in detail the genuine need for a post office or substation in the area. Letters of endorsement from political and other community leaders have also been submitted as a means to support the initiative. In addition, face-to-face meetings were held with her in order to convey how important the initiative was to the area.

I will not ask the Ouachita Parish Tax Collection office to apologize for bungling up my property tax payment for 2006. The Parish's Assessor approved a homestead exemption for my house effective January 1, 2006. However, when the payment document was submitted to me, they failed to consider the exemption approval. The office was contacted and advised of the oversight and they promised that an amended billing statement would be submitted prior to the due date. The amended bill was not received by December 26, 2006. Consequently, I made the adjustment myself by deleting the amount associated with non-exemption for homesteading with my payment submitted on December 26. On January 4, 2007, the tax collection office called to inform me that I had committed a cardinal sin by changing the amount to be paid for property taxes. They asked that I come down to the office, pick up and void the check I had written and write another check to cover for taxes owed on the non-homestead property. They informed me that an amended property tax bill would be sent to me for the homestead exemption before the end of January 2007. As it turned out, I did not get an amended tax bill in January. It was received on February 10. Most businesses would have accepted the first check that was written and subsequently billed or refunded the difference between the amount of the check and the actual amount owed to them. As I had anticipated, the final amount owed was the same as shown on my original check dated December 26, 2006. No apology was offered by the Assessor's office for the mistake and inconvenience.

I will not ask Chase Bank (Banc One Securities Corporation) and its broker for an apology for causing the Internal Revenue Service (IRS) to send me a notice for payment for an increase in federal tax liability ... not once but twice. On the first notice I received from IRS, Chase Bank acknowledged making an error (no apology) in processing the security transactions and reimbursed me for the amount I had to pay IRS for the oversight. However, Chase Bank officials refused to show ownership for the cause of the second notice, which was similar in nature to the first one. Chase Bank officials wrote to advise me that the organization does not summarize cost basis information during any given year for securities purchased. The letter further stated that it was the responsibility of clients to maintain cost basis information through statements and confirmations they routinely provided during the time of the transactions. However, what the letter and Chase officials failed to say was that the broker processed each transaction as a new purchase of securities rather than an exchange of same. I also learned after communication with IRS that a security exchange document should have been prepared and filed by Chase's broker for most of the transactions. Undoubtedly, the processing of securities as new purchase transactions opposed to an exchange is much more favorable for a broker as well as for the corporation … financial-wise.

I will not ask the U.S. Representative from Alabama to apologize for carrying out a conspiracy theory to falsely implicate me at Central Alabama Veterans Health Care System (CAVHCS) in the late 1990s. The Congressman was in a position with the "power to hurt" as Chairman of a Subcommittee that had investigation and oversight authority on VA's operations. With this authority, he and members of his staff employed assistance from the VA's Office of Inspector General, VA's Office of General Counsel, Office of Special Counsel, General Accounting Office, Office of Personnel Management, Federal Bureau of Investigation, certain officials in VA Headquarters, a handful of employees at the Montgomery and Tuskegee campuses, the Montgomery County Republican Club, and the Alabama Republican Congressional delegation as a means to substantiate the false allegations. All of the above groups acquiesced with the plot except the Office of Special Counsel and Senator Richard Shelby. Unknowingly to most of us at the time, the conspiracy was initiated long before the Secretary of VA considered approval of the merger of the two medical centers and creation of the Health Care System Director's position at CAVHCS. During a stakeholders' briefing in the summer of 1996, officials of the Montgomery County Republican Club asked the Atlanta Network Director to preclude my applying for and appointment to the position. The request was made to a large degree because the Director at the Montgomery medical center had announced his retirement. The VA Secretary approved the merger in September 1996. Through it own investigation the Office of Special Counsel found the underlining reason for the Office of Inspector General's review ... the conspiracy. Undoubtedly, the Congressman and his staffers have not read about former Congressman and President James Madison who felt that those who have a little power will always be tempted to abuse it and that they can be restrained only if they are kept under watchful eyes. The entire true story is described in another book entitle, "Conspriacy to Injustice."

I will not ask any of the above groups' members to apologize for not revealing the truth about how the integration was being implemented. All of them knew they were wrong and probably regretted it afterward.

I will not ask any of the individuals and/or organizations that failed to respond to the support group that wrote to them on my behalf and requested assistance. The requests were submitted shortly after the Alabama Congressman and VA's Office of Inspector General had undertaken inappropriate and conspiracy actions against John Hawkins and myself at Central Alabama Veterans Health Care System. The individuals and organizations who failed to not only respond but did not acknowledge receipt of the requests for assistance were: Former President Bill Clinton, Congresswoman Maxine Waters, Congressman Jesse Jackson, Jr., Attorney Vernon Jordan, Former First Lady, Hillary Clinton, Congress on Racial Equality (CORE), Black in Government (BIG), Rainbow Coalition, National Association for the Advancement of Colored People (NAACP), National Urban League, Inc., Southern Christian Leadership Conference (SCLC). The Congressional Black Caucus is the only organization that responded to the support group's inquiry. However, instead of reviewing the information package material sent to them, the Congressional Black Caucus sent the inquiry to the subject Alabama Congressman for a response. Even more asinine was the fact that the Caucus sent the Alabama Congressman's reply they received from him directly to us as their response to the issue. Evidently, this was a learning experience for me. I learned that if a person get into a situation similar to the one described in the book, "Conspiracy to Injustice," and not have sufficient resources to defend him or herself, he or she might find himself/herself in jail for an offense he/she did not commit.

I will not ask officials from NewSouth Books Publishing Company in Montgomery, Alabama to apologize for procrastinating for more than two years on the publication of my book, "Conspiracy to Injustice." The manuscript was retracted and submitted to another publisher because of the unreasonable and unexplained delay. Suspicions surrounding why the publication was delayed were never resolved.

References

Eileen R. Borris-Dunchunstang, Ed. D., Finding Forgiveness: A 7-step Program for letting go of anger and bitterness. (McGraw-Hill, New York, 2007)

Harriette Cole, How to Be Contemporary Etiquette for African Americans. (Simon & Schuster, Inc., New York, 1999)

Peter Post, Essential Manners for Men: What to do, When to do it, and Why. (Harper Resource, New York, 2003)

Beverly Engel, Power of Apology: Healing Steps to Transform all Your Relationships. (John Wiley & Sons, Inc., New York, 2001)

Peggy & Peter Post, The Etiquette Advantage In Business. (Harper Collins Publishers Inc., New York, 2005)

Webster's New World Dictionary, Third College Edition. (Simon & Schuster, Inc., 1988)

Marsha L. Wagner-Columbia University, "All I want is For Him to Apologize To Me ." (California Caucus of College and University Ombudsman; UCI Ombudsman: The Journal, 1996, Updated: February 21, 1997)

Free Press, (Newspaper). (Monroe, LA, December 23, 2006)

Associated Press, Headquarters. (New York, NY, March 2007)

Leonard P. Ullmann & Leonard Krasner, A Psychological Approach to Abnormal Behavior. (Prentice-Hall, Inc., Englewood Cliffs, New Jersey, 1969)

Ken Dooley, "The Good Stuff." (Progressive Business Publications, Malvern, PA, 2007)

Fred D. Gray, The Tuskegee Syphilis Study. (NewSouth Books, Montgomery, AL, 1998)

Good News Bible, The Bible in Today's English Version (American Bible Society, New York, 1976)

William Greider, Secrets of The Temple: How the Federal Reserve Runs The Country. (Simon & Schuster, Inc., New York, NY, 1989)

Jimmie L. Clay, FACHE, Conspiracy to Injustice and Web page, Conspiracytoinjustice.com. (1st Books Library, Bloomington, IN., 2003)

Glossary

Aberration. A departure from what is right, true, correct, etc.

Abnormal. Not normal; not average; not typical; not usual; irregular, esp. to a considerable degree.

Accost. To approach and speak to; greet first, before being greeted, esp. in an intrusive way.

Acknowledge. Declare to be true or admit the existence or reality or truth of something.

Adversarial. Relating to a situation in which two parties are hostile opponents.

Affront. To insult openly or purposely; offend; slight. To confront defiantly.

Alienate. To make unfriendly; estrange. 'His behavior alienated his friends.'

Apologize. To make an apology; acknowledge, and express regret for, a fault, wrong, etc.

Apology. To speak in defense. An acknowledgment of some fault, injury, insult, etc., with an expression of regret and a plea for pardon.

Anthropology. The study of humans, esp. of the variety, physical and cultural characteristics.

Anti-Semite. An anti-Semitic person.

Anti-Semitic. Having or showing prejudice against Jews.

Arrogant. Full of or due to unwarranted pride and self-importance. Over-bearing.

Behave. To conduct (oneself or itself) in a specified way; act or react.

Behavior. The way a person behaves or acts; conduct, or manners.

Behavior Scientists. Professionals in areas such as sociology, psychology, anthropology and social work who examine human activities in an attempt to discover recurrent patterns and to formulate rules about social behavior.

Cardinal Sin. Highest offense against God, religion, or good morals.

Catholic. The Christian church as a whole; specifically, of the ancient undivided Christian church. The Christian church headed by the pope; Roman Catholic.

Cavalier. Free and easy. Casual or indifferent toward matters of some importance.

Celebrity. A famous or well-publicized person. Multitude, fame, with wide recognition; renown.

Christian. A person professing belief in Jesus as the Christ, or in the religious based on the teachings of Jesus.

Civil Rights. Rights guaranteed to the individuals by the 13th, 14th, 15th, and 19th Amendments to the Constitution of the United States and by other acts of Congress; esp., the right to vote, exemption from involuntary servitude, and equal treatment of all people with respect to the enjoyment of life, liberty, and property and to the protection of law.

Confession. An admission of guilt, esp. formally in writing, as by a person charged with a crime.

Conspiracy. A planning and acting together secretly, especially for an unlawful or harmful purpose such as plotting to remove a person from office.

Constituents. That can or does appoint or vote for a representative, esp. from a certain area.

Contentment. The state, quality, or fact of being satisfied.

Contrition. Remorse for having done wrong.

Criticize. To analyze and judge as a critic. To judge disapprovingly; find fault.

Damage. Injury or harm to a person or thing, resulting in a loss in soundness or value.

Defense. The act or power of defending, or guarding against attack, harm, or danger.

Demand. To ask for boldly or urgently. To ask for as a right or with authority. To order to appear; summon.

Deviance. Deviating (as to turn aside), especially from what is considered normal in a group or for a society. A person whose behavior is deviant.

Diplomacy. The conducting of relations between people and nations. Skill in dealing with people. Tact.

Disparage. To marry one of inferior rank. To lower in esteem; discredit. To speak slightingly of. Show disrespect for; belittle.

Disrespect. To have or show lack of respect for or esteem. Discourtesy.

Diversity. The quality, state, fact or instance of being difference. Unlikeness. Variety; multiversity.

Embarrass. To cause to feel self-conscious, confused and ill at ease. Disconcert. To cause difficulties to. Hinder. Impede.

Empathy. The projection of one's own personality into the personality of another in order to understand the person better.

Epithet. That which is added, a disparaging one, used to characterize some person or thing. Examples: A black-hearted villain, Ivan the Terrible.

Etiquette. The forms, manners, and ceremonies established by convention as acceptable or required in social relations, in a profession, or in official life.

Exacerbate. To make more intense or sharp; aggravate (disease, pain, annoyance, etc.).

Forgive. To give up resentment against or the desire to punish; stop being angry with a person or group. Excuse a fault or offense.

Forgiveness. A forgiving or being forgiven. A pardon.

Gesture. Anything said or done to convey a state of mind, intention, etc.; often, something said or done merely for effect or as a formality. A movement, or movements collectively, of the body, or of part of the body, to express a emphasize ideas, emotions, etc.

Humiliate. To hurt the pride or dignity of by causing to be or seem foolish or contemptible.

Ignorant. Having little knowledge, education, or experience of a particular area or matter.

Inconsiderate. Without thought or consideration for others. Ill-advised.

Insane. Mentally ill or deranged. Very foolish, impractical.

Insensitive. Incapable of being impressed, influenced, or affected; having little or no reactions.

Islam. The Muslim religion, a monotheistic religion in which the supreme deity is Allah and the chief prophet and founder is Mohammed.

Insult. To leap upon, scoff at. To treat or speak to with scorn, insolence, or great disrespect. A remark, etc. that hurts or is meant to hurt the feelings or pride on someone or group. To behave arrogantly toward someone else.

Jim Crow. Traditional discrimination against or segregation of blacks, esp. in the U.S.

Manipulate. To manage or control artfully or by shrewd use of influence, often in an unfair or fraudulent way.

Manners. Ways or methods in which some things are done or happen; mode or fashion of procedures.

Micromanage. To conduct, carry on, or have under control at the highest level. Maintain supervisory control of operations of a business at the top level or from outside the organization or group.

Motive. Some inner drive, impulse, intention, etc. that causes a person to do something or act in a certain way; incentive; goal.

Muslim. An adherent of Islam.

Obscene. Offensive to one's feelings, or to prevailing notions, of modesty or decency; lewd.

Offensive. Attacking; aggressive. Of or for attack. Causing resentment, anger, etc.; insulting.

Ombudsman. A person employed by an institution to investigate complaints against it. A public official appointed to investigate citizens' complaints against government agencies or officials that may be infringing on the rights of individuals.

Overt. Not hidden; open; observable, apparent; manifest.

Paparazzo. Photographers, esp. freelance ones, who take candid shots, often in an intrusive manner, of celebrities for newspapers and magazines.

Pardon. To release a person from further punishment for a crime. To forgive a person for some minor fault, discourtesy, etc.

Placebo. A harmless, unmedicated preparation given as a medicine to a patient merely to humor him, or used as a control in testing the efficacy of another, medicated substance.

Pomposity. The quality of being pompous; ostentation; self-importance.

Presumptuous. Too bold or forward; taking too much for granted; showing over-confidence, arrogance, or effrontery.

Psychology. The science dealing with the mind and with mental and emotional processes.

Regret. To feel troubled or remorseful over something that has happened, one' own acts, etc. To feel sorry about or mourn for a person or thing gone, lost, etc.

Rehabilitate. To restore to a normal or optimal state of health, constructherapy. To restore to rank privileges, or property which one has lost. To restore the good name or reputation of; reinstate in good repute.

Remorse. A deep, torturing sense of guilt felt over a wrong that one has done.

Reparation. A repairing or being repaired; restoration to good condition. A making of amends; making up for a wrong or injury.

Revenge. To inflict damage, injury, or punishment in return for (an injury, insult, etc.); retaliates for.

Social Work. Any service or activity designed to promote the welfare of the community and the individuals, as through counseling services, health clinics, etc.

Social Worker. A person trained to perform the tasks of social work, esp. one who holds a college or university degree in social work.

Sociology. The science of human society and of social relations, organization, and change; especially the study of the beliefs, values, etc. of societal groups and of the processes governing social phenomena.

Soiree. At a late hour. A party or gathering in the evening.

Sorry. Feeling or expressing regret or a sense of loss over something done or not done.

Sterilization. To make incapable of producing others of its kind, as by removing the organs of reproduction or preventing them from functioning effectively.

Syphilis. An infectious venereal disease caused by a spirochete (Treponema palidum) and usually transmitted by sexual intercourse or acquired congenitally: if untreated, it can ultimately lead to the degeneration of the heart, bones, nerve tissue, etc.

Ulterior. Lying beyond or on the farther side. Beyond what is expressed, implied, or evident; undisclosed as an ulterior motive.

Why Apologize?

◆

(Taken From Why Worry?)

There are only two things to consider about apologizing; either you were considerate or inconsiderate of the offended person.

If you were considerate, then there is nothing to apologize for. But if you were inconsiderate, there are two things to be concerned about; either you apologize or you do not apologize.

If you apologize in an appropriate and meaningful way, then there is nothing else you need to do. If you do not apologize, there are two things to consider; either you reconsider and apologize or evade the issue and spend the rest of your life being recognized as an inconsiderate bonehead.

If you repent as an inconsiderate bonehead and apologize there is nothing else you need to do. But if you decide to spend the rest of your life recognized as an inconsiderate bonehead, you will not get too far in this world.

About the Author

Jimmie L. Clay, FACHE, is a retired VA Healthcare System Director with more than 33 years of leadership service. He has a Bachelor of Science degree in Business Administration and a Masters degree in Management/Human Relations & Organization Behavior with specialization in healthcare management. He successfully directed the activities at the Tuskegee VA Medical Center for more than twelve years and served as Health Care System Director for the integration of the Montgomery and Tuskegee VA Medical Centers for two years. He is a Fellow in the American College of Healthcare Executive, a professional organization whose mission includes promotion of high ethical standards of conduct. He was selected to represent VA on the prestigious president's Task Force on National Health Care Reform and was commended for his performance.

Index

978-0-595-46096-0
0-595-46096-8